SWEDISH COOKING

© 1971 ICA-FÖRLAGET AB, VÄSTERÅS, SWEDEN
2nd edition
ICA Test Kitchen: Swedish Cooking
Recipes selected by Asta Östenius and Brita Olsson
Text and translation: Görel Kristina Carheden
Photographs: Stig-Arne Holm, Esselte foto, Stockholm;
     Hans von Sterneck, Stockholm;
     Olle Åkerström, Ateljé Bogstedt, Stockholm.
Cover: Paul Hilber, Stockholm.
Printed by Palmeblads Tryckeri AB, Göteborg, Sweden 1973

ISBN 91-534-0024-0

CONTENTS

FOREWORD

Visiting a foreign country — either for a shorter or longer time — one soon notices that lots of things are different from what one is used to. Foods and eating habits for example differ quite a bit from country to country.

To cook in a foreign country with new foreign foods can be an exciting adventure. It is fun to try the specialties of the country in one's own kitchen. Or just to read about what goes into the new dishes one meets.

This book is meant as a guide to Swedish food today. "Swedish Cooking" gives more than a hundred recipes characteristic of Swedish food, both the everyday kind and the more festive fare. To make it easier to use the recipes, the ingredients are given in ounces and cups as well as in grams and deciliters.

Brown beans, pea soup and many other traditional Swedish **husmanskost** dishes take a long time to prepare. You can now buy these dishes ready-cooked in the supermarkets. This book includes a list of commonly available convenience foods; use it to choose typical Swedish foods that you want to taste or to take back home with you.

Good food, plenty of good food, has always been part of Swedish holiday celebrations. In this matter, Swedes are very tradition-bound. Everyone must have **lutfisk** on Christmas Eve. Or Fat Tuesday Buns during Lent and gaily colored eggs at Easter. Many dishes, such as cheese cake, potato dumplings and **glödhoppa,** are typical of a special province. The book will tell you more about all this.

Going to a Swedish dinner party may bring on problems for the uninitiated guest from another country. The chapter on Swedish etiquette gives some good advice for when you are a guest, as well as when you are a host or hostess, in Sweden. You will also find here the rules for how to handle the smörgåsbord. Finally, the book leaves you a few menus for typical Swedish meals, everyday family-type meals and more festive meals. The recipes for the dishes suggested in these menus are all included in the book.

Ginger Snaps (p. 99) can be made at any time of the year, but the frosting decorations and the characteristic, traditional cookie forms are used only at Christmas.

THINGS
TO
REMEMBER
WHEN
USING THIS BOOK

All recipes yield 4 servings when not otherwise indicated.
All measurements are level.

The measures used in Sweden are deciliter (dl) and grams (g). The standard set of measuring spoons includes tablespoon, teaspoon and **kryddmått** or spice spoon. Use the following table to translate Swedish measurements into the nearest convenient American equivalent and vice versa. (The British fluid ounce is 1.04 times the American ounce).

1 dl = 100 milliliter (ml) or fluid grams = $6^2/_3$ tablespoons = $3^1/_2$ fluid ounces
1 liter =10 dl = 1 fluid kilogram (kg) = 2.2 fluid pounds
1 spice spoon = 1 ml
1 teaspoon = 5 ml = $^1/_6$ fluid ounce
1 tablespoon = 15 ml = 3 teaspoons = $^1/_2$ fluid ounce
1 U.S. cup= 8 fluid ounces = 227 ml or 2.27 dl
1 pound (lb) = 16 ounces (oz) = 454 g
1 ounce = 28.35 g
1000 g = 1 kilogram (kg)
To convert grams to ounces, multiply the grams by 0.035

Miscellaneous Measures

	dl	tablespoon
Cocoa	40 g	
Coffee	40 g	
Farina	70 g	
Graham flour	60 g	
Macaroni	50 g	
Margarine and butter, cold		15 g
Margarine and butter, melted	90 g	13 g
Nuts, shelled	65 g	
Oil	90 g	13 g
Oat meal	35 g	
Potato starch flour	80 g	12 g
Powdered sugar	60 g	
Raisins	60 g	
Rice	85 g	
Rye flour	55 g	
Salt	125 g	19 g
Sugar	85 g	
Syrup	140 g	
Wheat flour	60 g	9 g

Flour used in the recipes is always Swedish all-purpose wheat flour except when otherwise indicated.

Swedish spirit vinegar (12% acidity), Swedish syrup, lingonberry and cloudberry preserve, potato starch flour, pearl sugar and vanilla sugar may be obtained in Scandinavian delicatessen in the United States.

Baking always takes place in a preheated oven.

All temperatures are told in ° Celsius (Centigrade).

To convert Celsius into Fahrenheit, multiply by 9, divide by 5, and add 32.
To convert Fahrenheit into Celsius, subtract 32, multiply by 5, and divide by 9.

Conversion Table (rounded figures)

°Celsius	°Fahrenheit	
100 to 150	212 to 300	slow oven
175 to 225	350 to 425	moderate hot oven
250	475	hot oven
275	525	very hot oven

Can sizes

Fish, vegetables, fruit:

$1/1$-can contains about 8 dl = 800 g
$1/2$-can   ,,   ,,   4 dl = 400 g
$1/4$-can   ,,   ,,   2 dl = 200 g

Soups:

Soup cans come in two sizes; the family-size can contains about 1 liter, the smaller can about 6 dl.

Meat:

Large $1/2$-can contains about 500 g
Large $1/3$-can   ,,   ,,   300 g
Mushrooms also come in $1/8$-cans which contain about 100 g.

Can sizes refer to Swedish standard sizes.

How much?

Fish:

Whole cleaned fish	200 to 250 g per serving
Fish, cut in slices	150 to 200 g per serving
Fish fillets	100 to 150 g per serving

Meat:

Meat with bones	150 to 250 g per serving
Boneless meat	100 to 150 g per serving
Ground meat	75 to 100 g per serving
Salt pork	75 to 100 g per serving
Bacon	50 to 75 g per serving
Ham, cooked or smoked ..	75 to 100 g per serving

11

Miscellaneous:

Cheese for sandwiches....	20 g per serving
Cheese for cheese tray ..	50 to 100 g per serving
Butter or margarine for the table	10 to 15 g per serving
Creamed or melted butter or margarine	20 to 25 g per serving
Mayonnaise, 1 to 2 table-spoons or...............	15 to 30 g per serving

SWEDISH FOOD TRADITIONS

Genuine Swedish food — is there such a thing? Tournedos, paella, hamburgers ... the food served in Swedish homes and restaurants often has a foreign flavor as a result of the Swedish love of travel.

But Sweden does indeed have a fine old culinary tradition rich in native dishes. The Swedish **husmanskost,** good old everyday Swedish food based on classic country cooking, has admittedly been influenced by foreign cuisine over the years. Basically, however, it is genuinely Swedish. Today, the plain and hearty husmanskost is undergoing a renaissance in Sweden. The best of the old recipes have been revived and in many cases revised so that they are less sturdy, simpler to prepare and better suited to modern way of living without having lost any of their special charm and characteristics. Propaganda for better diets has also helped to improve the Swedish husmanskost by a reduction of the fat content matched by an addition of fresh fruit and vegetables.

The Swedish Smörgåsbord

The Swedish smörgåsbord is world famous. Today, however, the traditional large smörgåsbord with its lavish array of food can be found only in a few restaurants, usually at Christmas time. A much reduced version of the smörgåsbord is sometimes served in the homes, also usually at Christmas time. Once in a while, mostly in rural areas, the complete old-time smörgåsbord will be prepared. When you meet with a smörgåsbord of this kind, it is important to know the rules for how to approach it, or it may become just a hotchpotch of flavors and impressions.

The commonly accepted and best way of enjoying the large smörgåsbord is to eat each kind of food separately, changing to a clean plate whenever it is deemed necessary. Never try to sample everything but take a little of each of your favorite dishes. Start with the herring and let it be accompanied by a potato, crispbread and butter. When you have relished this, go back for some smoked, pickled or poached fish. Return to the smörgåsbord and help yourself to your favorites among the cold cuts and salads. Then sample the hot dishes. Finally have some cheese and fruit and, if desired, dessert and coffee. Remember that you are free to take as many trips to the smörgåsbord as you want to, but never load your plate with too many various foods at the same time.

A small smörgåsbord consisting of a few herring dishes, hot boiled potatoes, butter, cheese and crispbread is often served as an appetizer before dinner. Sometimes this smörgåsbord may be extended with a few more dishes and served for a late supper. A medium large smörgåsbord is often a practical form of buffet-style entertaining. In the chapter on menus you will find suggestions for a smörgåsbord.

The Swedish Sandwich

Bread, butter and cheese are often served with the meal in Sweden. Everyone makes his own open-face sandwich which is eaten whole, either before, during or at the end of the meal — the sandwich is not broken or cut in pieces. Foreigners in Sweden are often astonished to see large sandwiches being eaten out of the hand without using a fork and knife but this is the fully accepted way of eating any sandwich so prepared to make it practical. Danish style sandwiches or **smörrebröd** consisting of a single thin slice of bread generously covered with meat, fish or cheese and appropriate garnish are quite popular in Sweden; served on festive occasions, this kind of sandwiches are always eaten with a fork and knife.

For a large part of the Swedish people, sandwiches often make the whole lunch or supper. The ingredients may be then be served separately or as ready-made sandwiches. For the everyday sandwich, crispbread is a must. This Swedish specialty comes in different shapes, from the large round cakes with or without a hole in center to the smaller window-shaped pieces; and in various thicknesses, from the coarse thick rye crispbread to the thin white and brittle Norrland crispbread. The once so popular sweet **limpa** is slowly being replaced by more wholesome unsweetened bread. Sour dough bread baked of graham, dark rye or barley flour tastes wonderful together with good cheese and sausage, the two most common toppings for Swedish sandwiches.

The Swedish cheese industry offers good reproductions of foreign cheeses as well as a number of excellent native specialties. Here are the names of the most common Swedish cheeses. The figures mark the fat content : 60+ denotes a high fat content, 45+ a medium high and 30+ a low fat content.

Grevé (45+) resembles Swiss cheese with its sweet mild flavor.

Herrgårdsost (50+ to 30+) is usually sold aged. Fresh it has a mild round flavor.

Hushållsost (60+ to 30+) is a typical Swedish "country cheese" with a mild, slightly sour taste.

Kryddost (usually 30+) is flavored with caraway and cloves. A cheese men like.

From left to right, above: **frukostkorv** (breakfast sausage), **prinskorv** (prince sausage), femmarkerkorv, juniper-smoked **medvurst** and household medvurst. Next row: falu sausage, wiener sausage, falu sausage ring, **köttkorv** (meat sausage), **värmlandskorv** and **fläskkorv** (pork sausage).

Mesost (10+) is made from the whey obtained at cheese making. Brown, quite sweet. Children like it.

Prästost (50+ to 45+) is a fine old Swedish cheese with quite a strong flavor when well aged.

Sveciaost (60+ to 20+) is the most commonly sold cheese in Sweden. Fresh it has a mild flavor, when aged the taste becomes strong and sharp. Sometimes flavored with cloves and caraway.

Västerbottenost (50+) a juicy brittle cheese common on the smörgåsbord. When aged, its flavor is fresh, strong and sharp.

There are also many kinds of good Swedish sausages well worth trying. Very few today make their own sausage but many of the old provincial recipes are used by the meat packing plants and good sausages can be bought everywhere. Especially the juniper-smoked and sauna-smoked sausages have a rich flavor and are very popular. The following smoked sausages all make good toppings for sandwiches.

Femmarkerkorv has a hearty, slightly sour flavor.

Spickekorv resembles salami sausage but is saltier and includes yellow onion.

Herrgårdskorv or **Dalarökorv** has a rich, slightly sour flavor.

Boiled **medwurst** and **skinkwurst,** with pieces of cooked ham, also make good sandwich toppings.

FOOD
AND
FESTIVALS
IN
SWEDEN

Christmas

Slaughtering, beer brewing, cooking, baking, candle making — these were some of the holiday preparations common in the old rural household. Today most Swedes lead a comfortable urban life and practically the entire Christmas holiday may be bought ready-made at the store. Nevertheless, come December and a smell of cinnamon and saffron, candles and copper polish can be noticed in every Swedish home. At no other time do the Swedes take so much trouble in preserving old customs as at Jul and to do some of your own cooking and baking is part of the holiday fun.

Julafton, Christmas Eve, is the all-important day of feasting and gift-giving. Usually around 2 p.m. Jul lunch will be served in the kitchen buffet style. Once a lavish table crowded with heavy dishes hot and cold, this Jul smörgåsbord is now considerably cut down in size to better suit the modern way of living. One old-time dish, however, the Christmas ham, will probably always remain a part of the holiday fare. Many Swedes also insist on **dopp i grytan** or Dip in the Kettle for a complete Christmas Eve: slices of rye bread are immersed in hot bouillon and then enjoyed together with ham, pork sausage or butter. Beer is the common beverage with the smörgåsbord which usually ends with coffee and Christmas cookies.

After lunch begins the wait for Tomten, the Swedish Christmas goblin and gift-bringer. When Tomten has left and all the presents have been opened and admired, it is time for the traditional Julafton supper — **lutfisk** and rice porridge. The custom of eating lutfisk, dried codfish cured with lye, is said to date from the time when Sweden was a Catholic country. An old custom is to use the creamy white rice porridge as a means of divination. Bury a blanched almond in the porridge — the recipient will marry within the coming year. Add a bitter almond — spinsterhood is in store for you. A small shiny coin — you are sure to become rich. Tradition requires everyone to produce a poem before approaching the porridge; it does not have to have high literary pretensions but it must be original.

Christmas Eve Smörgåsbord
Glassblower's Herring p. 56 with Boiled Potatoes
Herring Salad p. 42
Jansson's Temptation p. 59
Meatballs p. 76
Liver Pâté p. 88
Ovenbaked Christmas Ham p. 87
Red Cabbage Salad p. 45
Bread, Butter, Cheese
Coffee with Almond Tarts p. 102 or Pepparkakor p. 99

Christmas Eve Supper
Lutfisk p. 72 with Boiled Potatoes, Green Peas and White Sauce
Rice Porridge with Milk p. 104.

Fat Tuesday Buns (p. 96) come in various forms: some have lids, covering a slice of almond paste and whipped cream, some are excavated and then filled again with a mixture of crumbs, whipped cream and almond paste.

Lent

To convert the Nordic people to Christianity was not an easy task for the French monks and English missionaries sent to Scandinavia around the year 1000. For one thing, the people could not understand the necessity of fasting during Lent, the forty-day period of quiet and abstinence decreed by the Catholic church. Legend has it that the Vikings grumbled, clanked their swords and behaved on the whole in such a threatening manner that the authorities found it best to ease the regulations and allow the people a hearty meal of salt pork every Tuesday.

It is now more than 400 years since Sweden converted to the Protestant church but the tradition of having a heavy meal on Tuesdays during Lent is still observed. Fried salt pork with brown beans is the customary fare followed by a sturdy dessert called Fat Tuesday Buns, wheat-flour buns filled with almond paste, topped with whipped cream and served floating in a bowl of hot milk.

Lent Dinner
Fried Salt Pork with Brown Beans p. 53

*

Fat Tuesday Buns p. 96

Lady Day

A survivor from Catholic times, Lady Day or Annunciation Day remained a legal holiday on the Swedish calendar until 1952. Since then, Lady Day has been observed on the Sunday closest to the old date,

March 25th. Through dialectic corruption, the old Swedish name for Lady Day, **Vårfrudagen** became **Våfferdagen** and later **Våffeldagen** meaning Waffle Day. Thus was born the custom of having waffles for dessert on Lady Day.

Lady Day Dinner
Ovenbaked Pike p. 72
Boiled Potatoes and Tossed Green Salad

*

Crisp Waffles p. 92

Easter

Easter holiday means sunshine, snow, skiing, tulips, daffodils and budding birch twigs adorned with multicolored feathers. Easter is also little girls dressed to witches, a reminder of former times when the holiday was marked by a strong belief in dark superstitions. In the old days, Easter week even called for a special menu that included kale soup on Sheer Thursday, salt salmon pudding on Good Friday, and cooked eggs on Easter Eve. Today there are no set rules, but Easter Eve most Swedes will have a small smörgåsbord and cooked colored eggs are seldom missing. The Easter Sunday menu often includes a green soup and a pork or lamb roast.

Easter Sunday Dinner
Kale Soup p. 48

*

Roast Lamb p. 82
Hasselback Potatoes p. 51 and Tossed Green Salad

*

Vanilla Ice Cream with Cloudberry Preserve

Crisp Waffles (p. 92) with whipped cream and fresh cloudberries.

Midsummer

To Swedes from time immemorial Midsummer has always been a very special festival — a joyous celebration of summer, sunshine, youth and love. If you want to meet with the magic of the Nordic summer, go out into the country on Midsummer Eve. Join in the medieval ring dances around the Maypole, a tall mast covered with garlands of fresh field flowers and birch twigs. Or just listen to the gay old tunes from fiddle and accordion. Take a walk and breathe in the loveliness of the light summer night. Like everyone else you will forget to go to bed but stay up with the sun throughout the night.

Midsummer Day is usually celebrated with a dinner party outdoors. The traditional Midsummer menu includes salmon, chicken, new potatoes and fresh strawberries.

Midsummer Day Dinner

Smoked Warm Salmon Trout p. 69 or Gravlax with
Gravlax Sauce p. 67
Boiled New Potatoes

*

Fried Chicken p. 86
Tossed Green Salad or Mushroom Salad p. 44

*

Fresh Strawberries with Whipped Cream

Crayfish and surströmming

At the end of the summer, Swedes begin to look forward to the parties given in the honor of two seasonal delicacies — **kräftor** and **surströmming.** August 7th is the opening date for kräftor or crayfish. The small, black, fresh-water crustaceans are dropped live into boiling salted water with a huge bunch of dill; during cooking the crayfish, like the lobster, change their color to a bright red. After having been chilled for several hours, the crayfish are removed from the cooking liquid and piled in a huge mound on a platter decorated with fresh dill crowns. The ritual of crayfish eating is a wonderfully happy, noisy and messy shirt-sleeve affair; large bibs and paper napkins protect the diners as they do their best to suck out every morsel of meat and every drop of juice from the crayfish shell. A full August moon and gay paper lanterns complete the crayfish party which is usually held outdoors.

Surströmming, fermented Baltic herring, is in its own way just as dramatic a delicacy as crayfish. A specialty of northern Sweden, surströmming is for sale beginning the third Friday in August. To serve surströmming the proper way, tie a napkin around the can and place it on the table. Then carefully open the can — a strong odor will at once reach your nostrils and fill the room. Neophytes often need some time to get used to the unique smell of surströmming, some even go so far as to call it a stench. To seasoned surströmming lovers, however, nothing smells better than this little fish wich is always served with hot boiled potatoes, preferably **mandelpotatis,** the curved, oblong, yellow potatoes grown in northern Sweden. Thin white crispbread, also a Norrland specialty, butter and chopped yellow onion are the other accompaniments. Many like to make a **klämma** or surströmming sandwich: put butter, sliced potatoes and fillets of surströmming between two sheets of crispbread.

St. Martin's Day

Once upon a time there in the French town Tours a pious monk called Martin who was so much loved by the people that they wanted him to become their bishop. Martin, however, preferred to remain a monk and hid from his supporters in a flock of geese. Unfortunately the startled geese betrayed Martin by their vociferous gaggling. He was found and had to surrender. He took his revenge by deciding that every year on the day of his betrayal a goose should be killed and cooked for dinner. Ever since then November 11th, known as St. Martin's Day, has been celebrated with a goose dinner.

A legend is a legend is a legend. Certainly it is quite a coincidence that just at this time of the year the goose is nicely fattened and just right to slaughter. The tradition of having a goose dinner on St. Martin's Day spread north to Denmark and from there to Skåne, the Swedish province where people always have had an understanding for good food. Today **Mårten Gås** — a festive goose dinner on **Mårtens afton** or St. Martin's Eve November 10th — is a popular tradition among all Swedes. Still, it is only in Skåne that school children are given the day off. In a small family, a duck or a large chicken may be substituted for the goose, but whatever the bird, the frame around it is always the same. An authentic goose dinner starts with **svartsoppa** or black soup, a dark, velvety soup made of goose or pig's blood. This soup may be obtained ready-cooked in most grocery stores in November.

Mårten Gås Dinner

Black Soup

*

Roast Goose p. 86
Boiled or Baked Potatoes, Stewed Prunes and
Apples, Red Cabbage p. 53

*

Fresh Fruit

REGIONAL SPECIALTIES

On the whole, Swedes today all have the same food habits and customs. However, many provinces have a reputation for a special food or a local dish that may be prepared in the same way now as it was for hundreds of years ago. A trip through Sweden's twentyfour provinces can be an exciting culinary adventure. Let us start our tour in Skåne, Sweden's southermost province and the home of festive Mårten Gås dinners, lavish smörgåsbord luncheons and grand **ålagillen** or eel parties serving eel prepared in a dozen different ways. When in Skåne, remember to sample the **spettekaka,** the classic party cake of the province. Made of eggs, sugar and flour, the batter is slowly dropped onto a cone that rotates over open fire. After baking the tower-like cake is decorated with white frosting and adorned with flowers at the top.

Småland boosts its own famous dessert of nationwide popularity, the **ostkaka** or cheesecake. In the old days, ostkaka was served only on special occasions such as weddings, funerals and important holidays. The farm woman would wrap her ostkaka, made from numerous pints of milk and cream, in her best linen napkin, then wrap herself in her black

Ostkaka, Cheesecake from Småland (p. 102), served with fruit preserve.

Sunday silk scarf and be off for the party. Because all the women did the same thing, it could happen that 10 or 12 cheesecakes crowded the kitchen of the hostess. When it was time for dessert, every one of the cheesecakes had to be set out on the table. Good manners required that every guest sampled each ostkaka always starting at the center of the cake. Thus any leftover ostkaka could be filled with cream or fruit and served the following day as a "new" dessert. Today the food industry distributes ostkaka to all parts of the country and it has become an everyday dessert.

Småland and Öland are both known for their **kroppkakor,** dumplings made from raw as well as cooked potatoes, flour and salt. True kroppkakor are filled with cubed salt pork and allspice; boiled in water they are served steaming hot with lingonberry preserve and melted butter.

On the west coast, Halland and Bohuslän offer a wide variety of fish and shellfish prepared into hearty soups, salads and casseroles. If potato sausage is your dish, stop in Värmland and sample the true Värmland sausage made with beef, pork and cubed potatoes; when in Dalarna, try the local beef stew called **sö.** But if you are partial to lamb and mutton, go to Gotland and you will be treated to such good native dishes as **glödhoppa** — broiled slices of dried and salted lamb.

Along the coast of the Gulf of Bothnia, from Uppland to Norrbotten, the most important food is **strömming.** This small silvery fish, also called Baltic herring, is prepared with knowing hands into a multitude of different dishes, all delicious. Good salmon, trout, whitefish and whitefish caviar are other delights waiting for you in Norrland, the nine northern provinces of Sweden.

If you do not love fish, Norrland has still a lot to offer. You must try the dark, gamy reindeer meat from Lappland. Or the Västerbotten cheese, a smörgåsbord favorite. Or **åkerbär,** the rare exquisite berry that grows wild on short-stemmed plants along road-sides and ditches. The åkerbär looks like a small juicy raspberry but has an intensive, delightful aroma all its own. The **hjortron** or cloudberry is another fine Norrland fruit.

Two Norrland provinces, Västerbotten and Norr-botten, have their own famous dumplings, **palt.** Even more filling than kroppkakor, these dumplings, too, are served with butter and lingonberries. To enjoy palt best, do as the natives do and dig a hole in the dumpling, fill with butter. Then cut the palt in small pieces and dip into the well of quickly melting butter.

Other favorite Norrland specialties are **tunnbröd,** the thin white crispbread, and **fil-** or **långmjölk.** A lightly soured milk product, fil sometimes becomes so thick and "long" that a spoon dipped into it will come out perfectly clean, bright and shiny. Fil and tunnbröd are often combined into an old-time dish called **bryta** — fil mixed with small pieces of tunn-bröd. **Blöta** is the cold-weather dish — tunnbröd simmered in beef or pork bouillon and enjoyed hot with boiled pork or pork sausage.

SKÅL, TACK — SWEDISH CUSTOMS

Swedes have long had a reputation of being a stiff and formal people. Formerly, foreigners travelling in Sweden were often confused by the ceremonious drinking rituals and protocol of etiquette. But all this has changed. Modern Swedes are more and more doing away with the strict old rules. Extensive travelling has given them an international outlook and understanding of customs in other countries. Of course, older Swedes may still want to adhere to the proper etiquette and some are hurt when addressed with an improper **Du** or **Ni,** but, in general, everyone pays little attention to these things. However, for you who would like to know what is right behavior at dinner parties, here are a few things to remember.

When You are a Guest

Flowers to the hostess are always welcome. On formal occasions, the flowers are sent beforehand or afterwards with a thank-you-note.
After sitting down at the table, and wine has been

served, the host makes a short welcome speech and proposes a **skål;** one should not drink before this skål. Afterwards, everyone is free to drink by himself or to propose a skål as often as he wishes. It is only at very formal dinner parties that one never drinks except in the form of a skål. When there are more than six people at the table, one must never skål the host and hostess in order to spare them from drinking more than they want to.

This is the ritual of the formal skål. Someone proposes a skål with one or several persons. They all lift their glasses to "the third waistcoat button" and bow to each other, their eyes meeting. One sips the wine and lowers the glass back to the level of that same button while again meeting the eyes of the partner or partners. Another slight bow and the glasses are put back on the table.

Today, a skål is very often accompanied by just a friendly nod and a smile. Naturally, also those who are drinking non-alcoholic beverages may participate in a skål.

When the dessert has been served, the guest sitting to the left of the hostess thanks her for the good food from all of the guests; this may be done in the form of a little speech or simply be a few words of appreciation followed by a proposal of a skål for the host and hostess.

At a small dinner party, instead of a speech, it is customary that everyone personally thanks the host and hostess when the meal is over. Before leaving, one should again thank the host and hostess. If you

No Swedish dessert has so many variations as this season-bound delicacy, the Apple Cake. Another common form is described on p. 103.

want to be correct, do this before putting on your coat.

Sometimes during the week after the party, one may thank the host and hostess again by a written note or a telephone call. Although this is no longer a must, it is always nice for the hostess to hear from her guests in some way.

When You are the Host or Hostess

For a formal dinner party, written invitations are sent out at least 14 days beforehand and an answer is requested. In other cases, customs differ; invitations may be written or made over the telephone. Note that in Sweden an invitation is usually taken seriously. It is not as common as in the United States to say "You must come over and have dinner with us" without meaning anything more than a kind phrase.

Place cards are usually used only on formal occasions; guests are then seated according to age, rank, relationship etc. But very often one simply seats those guests together who one has reason to believe will enjoy each other. The hostess always has the male guest of honor as her partner; his place is to the left of the hostess. The host and his partner, the lady guest of honor, go first to the table while the hostess and her escort wait until last.

It is always nice if the host and hostess skål not only their partners but all of their guests. The guests will also appreciate if besides saying one is happy that they could come, one says thanks for the flowers or something else they brought with them.

A Swedish Smörgåsbord, including Meatballs (p. 76), Liver Pâté (p. 88), juniper-smoked medvurst, cold meat and Mushroom Salad (p. 44).

CONVENIENCE FOODS

Perhaps many will be searching this book for recipes for hip rose soup, liver dumplings or black soup. Why are not these old-time favorites included? The reason is that these and other good but time-consuming dishes are today produced by the Swedish food industry with an excellent result. Much of the good old husmanskost food is available fully or partly prepared; canned, frozen or freezedried.

Of course, to some the work preparing a certain favorite dish may be fun even if it takes time. Many times, however, it is a good idea to go half the way, that is, to use the industry product and season it with spices and other additions to suit the personal taste. Or you may cook one dish with great care and buy the rest of the food for the meal ready-made.

Some dishes are, of course, cheaper to make yourself than to buy. The difference is not very big, however, unless the household is very large. Today hardly anyone makes everything herself — bakes the bread, cooks the preserves etc. Also the housewife who does not work outside the home wants to use her time for other things than cooking and baking. Here follows a list of Swedish convenience foods.

Canned soups, large variety

Dried soup concentrates, large variety

Frozen fish soup (fisksoppa)

Frozen crêpes with mushroom filling (champinjon-crêpes)

Frozen crêpes with shellfish filling (skaldjurscrêpes)

Pickled herring (inlagd sill, glasmästarsill, löksill etc.)

Canned cooked strömming, herring, mackerel (makrill), cod roe (torskrom) and fish balls (fiskbullar)

Canned creamed crab (gräddstuvad krabba) and shrimps (gräddstuvade räkor)

Frozen fish balls (fiskbullar)

Frozen fish au gratin (fiskgratäng)

Frozen fish casseroles (kräfströmming, fisk i form, torskrutor etc.)

Frozen breaded fish sticks (fiskpinnar)

Frozen and canned meatballs (köttbullar)

Frozen and canned hamburgers

Frozen and canned beef stew (kalops)

Frozen and canned cabbage rolls (kåldolmar)

Frozen and canned veal with dill sauce (dillkött)

Canned spaghetti sauce (köttfärssås)

Canned hash (pytt i panna)

Canned sailor's beef casserole (sjömansbiff)

Frozen creamed liver (leverstuvning)

Frozen beef with horseradish sauce (pepparrotskött)

Frozen beef Stroganoff

Frozen beef à la Lindström

Instant mashed potatoes (potatismos)

Instant mashed rutabagas, swedes (rotmos)

Potato pancake mix (raggmunk)

Canned brown beans (bruna bönor)

Canned creamed asparagus (gräddstuvad sparris)

Canned creamed mushrooms (gräddstuvade champinjoner)

Frozen creamed spinach (stuvad spenat)

Fruit puddings (kräm), large variety
Fruit compotes (kompott), large variety
Chocolate pudding mix (chokladpudding)
Bavarian cream mix (fromage)
Vanilla sauce mix (vaniljsås)
Cake mix, large variety
Coffee bread mix
Pancake mix
Waffle mix
Scones mix
Frozen puff paste (petits-choux-deg)
Frozen puff pastry dough (smördeg)

SANDWICHES

The open-face Swedish sandwich varies in size from the tiny canapé to the giant many-sectioned sandwich that is a whole meal in itself.

Giant Gourmet Sandwich
Delikatesslandgång

1 slice white sandwich
bread, cut lengthwise
margarine or butter

I. 1 to 2 tablespoons
whipped cream
dill or parsley
1 slice smoked salmon

II. 1 small, curved, light
green lettuce leaf
1 tablespoon mayon-
naise
paprika
6 to 8 peeled shrimps
1 lemon wedge

III. 2 tablespoons liver
pâté or mushroom
paste
2 to 3 large slices
cooked chicken
sliced pimento or
tomato wedges

IV. 1 slice Swiss cheese
1 small triangle
Gorgonzola cheese
lettuce leaves or
2 to 3 radishes or olives
2 to 3 pretzel sticks

Trim the crust and spread the bread with margarine or butter. Mark the bread in four sections.

I. Mix the whipped cream with enough chopped dill or parsley to color it a pale green. Spoon the cream over the first section. Roll up the salmon and put on top. Garnish with a nice sprig of dill.

II. Cover the second section with lettuce. Season the mayonnaise with paprika and put on top. Garnish with the shrimps and lemon wedge.

III. Spread the third part with liver pâté or mushroom paste. Cover with sliced chicken. Garnish with pimento or thin tomato wedges and a small parsley sprig.

IV. Cover the fourth and last section with the two kinds of cheese. Garnish with lettuce leaves, radishes or olives and pretzels.

Three Small Sandwiches
Tre små smörgåsar

Three Small Sandwiches is a very Swedish way to start a dinner. Designed to stimulate the appetite this diminutive form of the famous smörgåsbord offers a selection of fish, meat and cheese arranged on small pieces of bread cut in various shapes. Here follows a suggestion for how these sandwiches may be prepared; just before the guests sit down, put one sandwich of each kind at each table setting.

Caviar and Egg

white unsliced sandwich bread
margarine or butter
salt or smoked cod roe caviar
chopped hard-boiled egg
dill

Slice the bread lengthwise and spread with margarine or butter. Trim the crust. Put caviar along the edges and sprinkle with chopped hard-boiled egg in center. Cut across the sandwich strip to make small oblong sandwiches. Garnish with dill sprigs.

Ham and Prunes

rye bread
margarine or butter
lettuce
sliced ham
pitted prunes
parsley

Slice the bread and cut in triangles. Spread with margarine or butter. Cover with lettuce and top with ham and prunes. Garnish with parsley.

Cheddar and Cucumber

white unsliced sandwich bread or rye bread
margarine or butter
thick slices cheddar cheese
cucumber

Slice the bread lengthwise and spread with margarine or butter. Trim the crust. Cover with cheese and cut in triangles or rectangles. Garnish with thinly sliced cucumber.

Open-faced sandwiches on crispbread or rye bread, covered with leek and grated carrots, medvurst and cheese or fruit and salad.

Caviar Canapé
Löjromssnitt

4 slices white sandwich
bread
margarine or butter
2 to 3 tablespoons finely
chopped chives
50 g (about 2 oz.) whitefish
caviar
1 lemon

Trim the crust. Spread the bread with margarine or butter and press into finely chopped chives. Cut in triangles. Put a dab of caviar in center of sandwich and garnish with a piece of lemon.

Variation: Instead of sandwich bread, **tunnbröd** or Norrland crispbread may be used.

Shrimp Sandwich
Räksmörgås

4 slices white sandwich
bread
4 lettuce leaves
4 hard-boiled eggs, sliced
400 g (14 oz.) fresh
cooked shrimps

DRESSING
2 tablespoons prepared
mustard
1 tablespoon red wine
vinegar
$^{1}/_{2}$ dl ($^{1}/_{4}$ cup) chili sauce
1 egg yolk
2 dl ($^{3}/_{4}$ cup) oil
salt and pepper

Trim the crust and cover the bread with lettuce and sliced eggs. Peel the shrimps and put on top. Beat together the ingredients for the dressing and pour over the shrimps. If desired, garnish with a few shrimps on top.

40

Herring Sandwich
Sillsmörgås

4 slices dark rye bread
margarine or butter
1 to 2 tablespoons
mayonnaise
curry powder
2 hard-boiled eggs,
chopped
lettuce
1 can herring tidbits in
tomato sauce
dill or chives

Spread the bread with margarine or butter. Season the mayonnaise with curry to taste and blend with the chopped eggs. Put a small lettuce leaf on each sandwich and cover with the egg mixture. Arrange the herring on top. Garnish with chopped dill and/or chives.

Lapp Sandwich
Lappsmörgås

6 to 8 eggs
1/2 dl (1/4 cup) water
1/4 teaspoon salt
white pepper
2 to 3 tablespoons
margarine or butter
4 large slices white
sandwich bread
margarine or butter
150 g (about 5 oz.) sliced
smoked reindeer meat
parsley

Beat the eggs lightly with a fork. If desired, add the water for softer eggs. Season with salt and a pinch of freshly ground white pepper. In a heavy-bottomed saucepan, melt the fat. Add the egg batter and cook over medium-low heat, continually stirring. When beginning to set, remove from heat and let cool.
Spread the bread with margarine or butter. Cover with the meat and put a generous spoonful of the cold scrambled eggs on top. Garnish with parsley.

Variation: Substitute dried beef for the reindeer meat.

SALADS

All of the salads presented here may be served as part of a smörgåsbord. The Herring Salad and West Coast Salad both make an excellent first course or late supper dish; the other salads may be served as accompaniments for a fish or meat dish.

Herring Salad
Sillsallad

---

2 to 4 fillets of salt herring
2 to 3 cold cooked
potatoes
2 pickled beets
1 large apple
1 pickled cucumber
100 to 150 g (3¹/₂ to 5 oz.)
cooked ham
1 to 2 tablespoons liquid
from pickled beets
white pepper
1 to 1¹/₂ dl (¹/₂ to ³/₄ cup)
whipping cream
1 hard-boiled egg
finely chopped parsley

Soak the fillets in lots of cold water for 6 to 8 hours. Cut the potatoes, beets, apple, cucumber, ham and herring in small cubes. Mix it all and combine with liquid from pickled beets and a little pepper. Whip the cream and fold into the salad. Transfer to a serving bowl and garnish with strips of finely chopped egg white, egg yolk and parsley. Or pack the salad in a bowl, then unmold and garnish.

West Coast Salad
Västkustsallad

200 g (7 oz.) fresh cooked
shrimps
1 fresh cooked lobster or
6 to 8 cooked sea-crayfish
or equivalent amount
canned shellfish
100 g (3¹/₂ oz.) raw
mushrooms
1 head lettuce
2 tomatoes
1 small can asparagus
and/or
1 small pkg frozen peas

DRESSING
2 tablespoons red wine
vinegar
salt, white pepper
6 tablespoons oil

Peel the shrimps. Pick the meat from the lobster or sea-crayfish; cut in small pieces. Slice the mushrooms and shred the lettuce. Cut the tomatoes in thin wedges. Mix all the ingredients.

Shake together the ingredients for the dressing, blend with the salad. Chill before serving. Serve the salad with toasted bread as a first course or as a luncheon or supper dish.

Tomato Salad
Tomatsallad

4 to 5 large tomatoes
1 medium yellow onion
finely chopped parsley

DRESSING
1 tablespoon red wine
vinegar
¹/₂ teaspoon salt
white pepper
2 teaspoons chervil
4 tablespoons oil

Cut the tomatoes with a sharp knife in very thin slices; arrange these in rows on a platter, one slice overlapping the other. Or dip the tomatoes in boiling water and peel before cutting in half, then remove the seeds. Chop the onion finely and sprinkle over the tomatoes. Beat together the ingredients for the dressing and pour over the salad. Chill. Sprinkle with chopped parsley immediately before serving.

Variation: Add 100 to 150 g (3¹/₂ to 5 oz.) sliced raw mushrooms to the salad. Or add sliced olives.

Cucumber Salad
Inlagd gurka

1 medium cucumber
(about 500 g or 1 lb.)

DRESSING
³/₄ dl (¹/₂ cup) Swedish
spirit vinegar
2¹/₂ dl (1¹/₄ cups) water
³/₄ dl (¹/₂ cup) sugar
finely chopped parsley

Cut the cucumber in thin slices. Mix the vinegar, water and sugar; set aside for a few minutes, stirring now and then till the sugar is dissolved. Pour the dressing over the cucumber and add a generous sprinkling of finely chopped parsley. Chill for about 2 hours before serving.

Mushroom Salad
Champinjonsallad

200 g (7 oz.) raw
mushrooms

DRESSING
1¹/₂ tablespoons red
wine vinegar
4 tablespoons oil
salt, white pepper

Trim and cut the mushrooms in thin slices. Mix the ingredients for the dressing and pour over the mushrooms. Leave to marinate for at least 1 hour; stir the salad now and then.

White Cabbage and Lingonberry Salad
Vitkålssallad med lingon

1 wedge white cabbage
(200 g or 7 oz.)
1 dl (¹/₂ cup) lingonberry
preserve

Shred the cabbage finely. Mix with the lingonberry preserve and chill before serving.

44

Red Cabbage Salad
Rödkålssallad

**1 wedge red cabbage
(200 g or 7 oz.)
1 dl (¹/₂ cup) apple sauce
(unsweetened or lightly
sweetened)
2 to 3 teaspoons grated
horseradish**

Shred the cabbage finely. Mix the apple sauce and grated horseradish; blend with the cabbage. Serve the salad well chilled.

Beet Salad
Rödbetssallad

**2 to 3 pickled beets
2 cold cooked potatoes
1 small apple, peeled
2 tablespoons thinly
sliced leek**

DRESSING
**1¹/₂ to 2 dl (³/₄ to 1 cup)
cream-fil or sour cream
2 tablespoons finely
chopped pickled
cucumber
prepared mustard, salt,
white pepper**

Dice the beets, potatoes and apple; mix with the leek. Flavor the cream with chopped pickled cucumber, mustard and spices. Blend the salad with the dressing. Chill before serving. If desired, garnish with thin rings of leek.

SOUPS

Compared with other European nations, Swedes cannot be called a soup-loving people. Still, a common lunch is a bowl of soup with a crispbread sandwich and cheese. At a formal dinner, soup is often the first course. And at least once a week, a rich hearty soup is served for supper in Swedish homes. Yellow pea soup and pancakes is the traditional Thursday supper since centuries back. During Catholic times, the heavy fare probably served to fortify the people before Friday which was fasting day. Sweden converted to the Lutheran church in the sixteenth century but the pea soup tradition is still cherished.

Yellow Pea Soup
Gul ärtsoppa

4 dl (1³/₄ cups) dried yellow peas
1 liter (4 cups) water
1 tablespoon salt
300 to 400 g (10¹/₂ to 14 oz.) lightly salted side pork or
1 small pork shank
1 pinch ginger, thyme or marjoram
water

Rinse the peas and let soak in the water with salt for 10 to 12 hours. Bring the peas to a boil in the same water they have been soaked in, add 1 liter water. Cover and cook rapidly for a few minutes. Skim off the shells floating on the surface. Add the whole piece of pork. Or cut the pork in cubes and add when the peas have cooked for 30 minutes.
Let the soup simmer for 1 to 1¹/₂ hours or till peas and pork are tender. Add more water to the soup if too thick. Season with salt, ginger, thyme or marjoram. Remove the pork, cut in cubes and return to the soup.

Cabbage Soup
Brynt vitkålssoppa

$^{1}/_{4}$ to $^{1}/_{2}$ head white
cabbage (about 500 g
or 1 lb.)
2 tablespoons margarine
or butter
1$^{1}/_{4}$ liter (5 cups) beef
bouillon
salt, white pepper

Trim the cabbage and shred or cut it in small even pieces. Discard the coarser parts. Melt the margarine or butter in a kettle, add the cabbage. Cook, stirring, over medium heat until the cabbage is nicely browned. Add the bouillon. Cover and let the soup simmer until the cabbage is tender: fresh summer cabbage 15 to 30 minutes, winter cabbage up till 1$^{1}/_{2}$ hours. Season with salt and pepper. Serve the soup with meatballs or pork sausage. The sausage may be cooked in the soup.

Variation: The cabbage may be cooked without browning; the soup will then be lighter and have a milder taste. Add, if you like, sliced carrots and leek to this soup.

Cauliflower Soup
Blomkålssoppa

4 medium potatoes
(300 g or about 10 oz.)
1$^{1}/_{4}$ liter (5 cups)
beef bouillon
1 cauliflower (about
500 g or 1 lb.)
2 tablespoons margarine
or butter
2 tablespoons flour
salt, white pepper
(nutmeg)
2 tablespoons finely
chopped parsley

Peel the potatoes and cut in slices or cubes. Let cook in the bouillon till tender. Add the cauliflower divided into florets; cook until soft. Stir together the margarine or butter and flour, add this to the soup and let cook for a few minutes. Season with salt, white pepper and, if desired, a pinch of grated nutmeg. Sprinkle the soup with chopped parsley.

Leek Soup may be prepared in the same way. Follow the recipe above but instead of cauliflower use 2 or 3 fat leeks. Rinse and trim the leeks, then cut in a little less than 1 cm thick slices.

Vegetable Soup
Grönsakssoppa

1 small cauliflower
2 dl (1 cup) fresh peas or
1 small pkg frozen peas
4 tender carrots
1 leek
8 dl (3½ cups) water
salt
4 to 5 dl (1¾ to 2 cups)
milk
2 tablespoons flour
2 tablespoons margarine
or butter
salt, white pepper
2 tablespoons finely
chopped parsley

Rinse and trim the vegetables. Divide the cauliflower into florets and cut the carrots in pieces. Cut the leek in thin slices. Let the vegetables cook in the water with salt until almost tender. Add the milk.
Stir together the flour and margarine or butter, add to the soup and cook for a few minutes. Season the soup to taste. Sprinkle with finely chopped parsley.

Nettle Soup
Nässelsoppa

2 liter (8 cups) young
tender nettles
1¼ liter (5 cups)
beef bouillon
2 to 3 tablespoons flour
2 tablespoons margarine
or butter
salt, white pepper
1 teaspoon chervil
finely chopped chives

Rinse the nettles well, let cook in the bouillon till tender. Strain and chop or grind the nettles finely. Return the nettles and cooking liquid to the kettle; bring to a boil. Stir together the flour and margarine or butter, add to the soup. Let cook for a few minutes. Season the soup to taste with salt, pepper, pounded chervil and chives. Serve with hardboiled eggs cut in half or poached eggs.
Spinach Soup and **Kale Soup** may be prepared in the same way. Frozen kale or spinach may be substituted for fresh.

Melon slices, red and white currants, cherries — the season's fruits make the best dessert when available.

Stromming Soup
Strömmingssoppa

1 leek
1 to 2 carrots
1 piece celery root
50 g (about 2 oz.)
margarine or butter
1 to 2 tablespoons flour
1 liter (4 cups) fish
bouillon or water
1 bay leaf
4 to 5 white peppercorns
1 tablespoon salt
300 g (10^1/$_2$ oz.) fresh or
frozen fillets of stromming
(Baltic herring)
(paprika, tomato sauce)
finely chopped chives

Trim and slice the leek and carrots, cut the celery root in small cubes. In a kettle, heat the margarine or butter. Add the vegetables and let cook for a few minutes. Sprinkle with flour. Add the fish bouillon or water and spices. Let the soup simmer, covered, till the vegetables are almost tender. Then add the fish fillets and allow the soup to simmer for a few minutes. Taste it and correct the seasoning. Add, if desired, paprika or tomato sauce. Sprinkle the soup with chopped chives.

Fresh large herring may be used instead of stromming.

Vegetable Soup (p. 48), followed by an Apple Cake (p. 103) with vanilla sauce or icecream make an appetizing late summer dinner.

VEGETABLE DISHES

Swedish cooking can be divided into two periods, before and after the Potato. For two centuries this tuber has been an all-important staple in the diet of the Swedish people. Today a wide variety of vegetables such as cabbage, carrots, corn, peas, leek, broccoli, brussels sprouts and spinach are popular, too, but potatoes are still served almost daily in many Swedish homes. Sweden has a number of good potato dishes but usually potatoes are served boiled in their jackets.

Boiled Potatoes Swedish Style

Nothing tastes better than Swedish Dill Potatoes: scrub small new potatoes clean and drop into boiling salted water together with sprigs of fresh dill. Cook, covered, over moderate heat till tender or about 15 minutes. Test with a toothpick. Drain off the water and let the steam disappear. Serve at once.

To cook the larger winter potatoes, select potatoes of the same size and scrub them clean. If desired, peel the potatoes before putting them in a kettle. Add water to cover and 3 tablespoons salt for each kg potatoes. Bring to a boil, cover and turn down the heat. Let simmer till tender or about 20 minutes. Drain well and let the steam disappear. Serve at once.

Creamed Potatoes
Råstuvad potatis

¾ kg (about 1 lb. 10 oz.)
potatoes
1 tablespoon margarine
or butter
4 dl (1¾ cups) milk
salt, white pepper
finely chopped parsley

Wash and peel the potatoes, cut in slices or cubes. In a kettle, bring the milk and margarine or butter to a boil. Add the potatoes and cook, covered, till tender. Season to taste with salt and pepper. Sprinkle with chopped parsley. Serve with fried meat and fish.

Hasselback Potatoes
Hasselbackspotatis

12 small oblong potatoes
salt
3 tablespoons margarine
or butter
3 tablespoons grated
cheese

Wash and peel the potatoes. Cut in thin slices without cutting quite through; the potato should remain whole at the bottom. If large potatoes are used, cut in half lengthwise and place cut side down before slicing. Put the potatoes sliced side up in a well buttered baking dish. Sprinkle with salt and dot with margarine or butter. Bake in a 225° oven for 20 minutes. Sprinkle with cheese and bake for another 20 minutes.

Potato Pancakes
Rårakor, raggmunkar

1 kg (2 lb. 3 oz.) potatoes
1½ teaspoons salt
½ dl (¼ cup) water
50 to 75 g (about 2 to 2½
oz.) margarine, butter or
bacon fat

Peel and grate the potatoes. Mix with salt and water. Drop the batter by large tablespoonfuls into a skillet with hot fat. Cook the pancakes over medium-high heat till crisp and brown on both sides. If possible, serve the pancakes directly from the pan with fried pork and lingonberry preserve.

Creamed Carrots
Stuvade morötter

500 to 600 g (1 lb. 1 oz.) to 1 lb. 5 oz.) carrots
water, salt

SAUCE
1 to 1¹/₂ tablespoons margarine or butter
3 tablespoons flour
3 to 4 dl (1¹/₂ to 2 cups) milk mixed with liquid from cooking the carrots
salt, white pepper
3 to 4 tablespoons finely chopped parsley

Peel and cut the carrots in cubes or slices. Cook in lightly salted water till tender. Drain well. In a saucepan, melt the margarine or butter. Stir in the flour. Add the milk and bring to a boil beating the sauce until smooth. Let cook for a few minutes. Season to taste with salt and pepper. Fold in the cooked carrots and parsley.

Instead of carrots, any kind of vegetables, e.g. peas, beans or white cabbage, may be used.

Mushroom Casserole with Sausages
Svamplåda med korv

one ¹/₄-can mixed mushrooms, drained
2 tablespoons margarine or butter
salt, white pepper

CUSTARD
4 teaspoons flour
4 dl (1³/₄ cups) milk
4 beaten eggs

6 to 9 Swedish prince sausages or small frankfurters
margarine or butter

Chop the mushrooms and sauté in the margarine or butter. Season lightly with salt and pepper. Transfer the mushrooms to a buttered baking dish.

To make the custard, stir the flour with part of the milk to a smooth batter. Bring the remaining milk to a boil, stir in the flour mixture. Cook for 3 minutes and then let cool. Add the eggs and mix well. Season with salt and pepper, pour the batter over the mushrooms. Bake for about 30 minutes in a 175 to 200° oven. Sauté the sausages in a little hot margarine or butter and arrange on top of the casserole in the shape of a "star". Serve with tomato sauce.

Brown Beans
Bruna bönor

4 dl dried brown beans
(about 350 g or 12 oz.)
1¼ liter (5 cups) water
1 teaspoon salt
2 to 3 tablespoons white
vinegar or red wine
vinegar
2 to 3 tablespoons syrup

Rinse the beans and soak in the water for 10 to 12 hours. Bring to a boil in the same water the beans have been soaked in, add salt and cook, covered, for 2 to 2½ hours. Season to taste with vinegar and syrup.
When a pressure cooker is used, reduce the water to 1 liter and cook for 25 to 30 minutes.

Red Cabbage
Rödkål

¾ kg (about 1 lb. 10 oz.)
red cabbage
2 to 3 tablespoons
margarine or butter
¼ to ½ dl (¼ cup) syrup
1 small yellow onion
2 to 3 tablespoons red
wine vinegar
1 to 2 apples, peeled and
cut in wedges
1 tablespoon salt
white pepper or allspice

Shred the cabbage finely. Melt the margarine or butter in a heavy kettle, add the cabbage and syrup. Let cook over medium heat for about 15 minutes, occasionally stirring. Grate the onion and add together with the vinegar and apples. Cook, covered, over low heat for about 1½ hours or till the cabbage is tender. Stir now and then so that the cabbage does not burn. Season to taste with salt and pepper or allspice.
Pressure cooker may be used for this dish; cook for about 15 minutes.

Pickled Stromming may be prepared in the same way as Pickled Salmon, mackerel or herring (p. 66).

HERRING
AND
FISH

Sweden, a country of close to 100.000 lakes, innumerable rivers and a long coastal line, has always made good use of its rich supply of fish and shellfish. Among the different kinds of fish available, herring has of old a special position, so that Swedes always differentiate between **sill** and **fisk** or herring and fish. Various preparations with salt and fresh herring are a must on the smörgåsbord.

A close relative to the herring is **strömming** or, as it is sometimes called, Baltic herring. This small silvery fish is a favorite food of the people along the east coast. In late summer, **surströmming,** fermented strömming, is enjoyed at special parties. **Gravlax,** salmon, cured with salt, sugar and dill, and **lutfisk,** ling cured with lye, are two other all-Swedish delicacies.

Salt Herring
Spicken sill

4 to 6 fillets of salt herring
2 to 3 tablespoons finely chopped chives
1 tablespoon finely chopped yellow onion

Soak the herring in lots of cold water for 1 to 2 hours. Drain and cut in 2 cm thick slices. Place on serving platter and sprinkle with chopped chives and onion. Serve with hot boiled potatoes and icecold sour cream. Or serve with creamed potatoes flavored with onion.

Pickled Herring
Inlagd sill

4 to 6 fillets of salt herring

DRESSING
1½ dl (¾ cup) sugar
1 dl (½ cup) Swedish spirit vinegar
2 dl (about 1 cup) water
5 coarsely crushed allspice
1 bay leaf
1 to 2 red onions, sliced
dill sprigs

Soak the herring in lots of cold water for 10 to 12 hours, or follow the directions on the package. Drain. Stir together the sugar, vinegar and water. Add the allspice, bay leaf and onion. Pour the dressing over the herring and refrigerate for a couple of hours. Then cut the herring in 1 cm thick slices, cover with dressing and garnish with red onion rings and dill sprigs.

Variation: Instead of allspice, add 1 teaspoon whole cloves and 5 crushed white peppercorns to the dressing. Bring to a boil, let cool and pour over the herring reserving about ½ dl (¼ cup). Refrigerate for at least 2 hours. Slice the herring and place in serving dish. Add the remaining dressing and garnish with red onion rings, cloves and dill.

Glassblower's Herring
Glasmästarsill

2 to 3 whole salt herrings

DRESSING
1½ to 2 dl (1¾ to 1 cup) sugar
1 dl (½ cup) Swedish spirit vinegar
2 dl (about 1 cup) water
1 bay leaf
5 whole allspice
a few carrot slices
a few leek slices
½ yellow onion, sliced

Clean the herring and soak in lots of cold water for 12 hours. Scrape the herring and rinse well. Cut across in 1½ to 2 cm thick slices.
Stir together the sugar, vinegar and water. Bring to a boil together with the allspice and bay leaf; let cool. Put the herring and vegetables in layers in a glass jar. Pour in the dressing which should cover the herring completely. Refrigerate for at least 24 hours before serving.

56

Rollmops
Rollmops

4 to 6 fillets of salt herring

FILLING
**1/2 teaspoon crushed
black peppercorns
1/2 teaspoon crushed
white peppercorns
1 red onion, finely
chopped
1/2 dl (1/4 cup) finely
chopped dill**

DRESSING
**1 dl (1/2 cup) Swedish
spirit vinegar
1 1/2 dl (3/4 cup) water
1 1/2 dl (3/4 cup) sugar
1/2 dl (1/4 cup) tomato
ketchup or chili sauce**

Soak the herring in lots of cold water for 10 to 12 hours, or follow the directions on the package. Drain. Stir together the ingredients for the filling and spread on top of the fillets. Roll up each fillet starting from the head end; secure the rolls with toothpicks. Place the rolls in a jar or bowl.

Bring the vinegar, water and sugar to a boil. Let cool and flavor the dressing with tomato ketchup or chili sauce. Cover the rolls with the dressing and refrigerate for at least 24 hours before serving. To serve, cut each roll in thin slices and garnish with red onion rings and dill sprigs.

Spice Herring
Kryddsill

**5 kg (11 lb.) fresh large
herring or stromming
Swedish spirit vinegar
water
300 g (10 1/2 oz.) salt
400 g (14 oz.) sugar
8 to 10 bay leaves
20 g (3/4 oz.) coarsely
crushed white pepper-
corns
20 g (3/4 oz.) coarsely
crushed allspice**

Remove the gills and, at the same time, the intestines except for the milt and roe. Cover the fish with vinegar and water; mix 1 part vinegar with 2 parts water. Refrigerate for 24 hours. Drain. Put the fish and the spices in layers in a large jar. Store the herring for 3 weeks before serving, stromming 1 week.

Matjes Herring
Matjessill

1 can matjes herring
1/2 dl (1/4 cup) chopped
chives
2 dl (about 1 cup) cream-
fil or sour cream

Drain the herring and cut in serving pieces. Slide a spatula under the herring and transfer to an oblong serving dish so that the fillets look whole. Chill and garnish with dill sprigs, if desired. Serve with hot new dill potatoes, chopped chives and cream-fil or sour cream. Sliced green pepper and sliced red or yellow onion may also be served with matjes herring.

Herring fried in foil
Sill i kapprock

4 to 8 fillets of salt herring
50 to 75 g (about 2 to 2 1/4
oz.) margarine or butter
2 hard-boiled eggs,
chopped
2 to 3 tablespoons finely
chopped dill

Soak the herring in lots of cold water for 10 to 12 hours, or follow the directions on the package. Put each fillet on a piece of aluminum foil or grease-proof paper. Dot with margarine or butter and sprinkle each fillet with chopped egg and parsley. Fold the paper or foil around the herring and put the parcels in a 200° oven. Bake for about 10 minutes. Instead of dill, chopped yellow onion may be used.

Fried Salt Herring with Onions and Cream Sauce
Stekt salt sill med lök och gräddsky

4 fillets of salt herring
1 dl (about 1/2 cup)
rye flour
or
1/2 dl (1/4 cup) fine dry
bread crumbs and
1/2 dl (1/4 cup) flour
margarine or butter
2 yellow onions, sliced
2 dl (about 1 cup)
light cream

Soak the fillets for 10 to 12 hours, or follow the directions on the package. Drain well. Dip the herring in rye flour or bread crumbs mixed with flour. Fry in hot margarine or butter till brown on both sides, transfer to serving platter. Then fry the sliced onions till a golden brown and spread on top of the herring. Add the cream to the skillet and bring to a boil, stirring. Serve the herring with the hot cream. Or serve the herring with white sauce made with milk and flavored with sautéed yellow onion.

58

Jansson's Temptation
Janssons frestelse

6 potatoes
2 yellow onions
1 can anchovy fillets
2½ to 3 dl (1¼ to 1½ cups) light cream
1 tablespoon margarine or butter

Peel the potatoes, cut in thin sticks or grate. Slice the onions. Drain the anchovies and cut in pieces. Put the potatoes, onions and anchovies in layers in buttered baking dish. The first and last layer should be potatoes. Dot with margarine or butter on top. Pour in a little of the liquid from the anchovies and half of the cream. Bake in a 200° oven for about 20 minutes. Pour in the remaining cream and bake for another 30 minutes or till the potatoes are tender. Serve as a first course or supper dish.

Herring au Gratin with Potatoes
Sillgratäng med potatis

4 to 6 fillets of salt herring
1 large yellow onion, sliced
3 tablespoons margarine or butter
1 leek, sliced
500 g (about 1 lb.) potatoes, peeled and sliced
2 tablespoons fine dry bread crumbs
2 dl (about 1 cup) light cream
1 dl (½ cup) milk
finely chopped dill

Soak the herring in lots of cold water for 12 hours. Sauté the onion in part of the margarine or butter. Place the potatoes, leek, herring and onion in rows in a buttered baking dish. Sprinkle with bread crumbs and dot with margarine or butter. Bake in a 200 to 225° oven for 20 minutes. Add the cream and milk. Bake for another 25 to 30 minutes. Sprinkle with chopped dill and serve hot.
Instead of raw potatoes, boiled potatoes may be used; then reduce the liquid and allow 20 minutes total baking time.

Fried Fresh Herring with Mustard
Senapsstekt sill

1 kg (2 lb. 3 oz.) fresh
herring
2 egg yolks
2 tablespoons prepared
mustard
2 tablespoons whipping
cream
1 dl (¹/₂ cup) fine dry
bread crumbs
margarine or butter

Clean and fillet the herring. Rinse well, drain and
sprinkle with salt. Stir together the egg yolks, mustard
and cream. Dip the herring into the batter, then into
the bread crumbs. Heat a skillet with margarine or
butter. When the foam subsides, add the herring and
cook over medium heat till golden brown on both
sides. Serve hot or cold.

Pickled Stromming
Gravad strömming

1 kg (2 lb. 3 oz.) whole
stromming or
600 g (1 lb. 5 oz.) fillets
of stromming
water
2 tablespoons salt and
¹/₂ dl (¹/₄ cup) Swedish
spirit vinegar for each
liter water

DRESSING
¹/₂ dl (¹/₄ cup) prepared
mustard
3 tablespoons sugar
1 teaspoon salt
1 teaspoon coarsely
crushed white pepper-
corns
1¹/₂ dl (³/₄ cup) oil
1 tablespoon spirit
vinegar
¹/₂ to 1 dl (¹/₄ to ¹/₂ cup)
finely chopped dill

Clean and fillet the fish. Remove the skin. (If this is
difficult to do, wait until the fish has soaked in the
vinegar for a while). Put the fillets in water mixed
with salt and vinegar for 1 to 2 hours. Drain. Stir
together the mustard, sugar, salt and pepper for the
dressing. Gradually add the oil, then the vinegar and
dill.
Put the fish and dressing in layers in a deep serving
dish. Refrigerate for at least 24 hours. Serve cold
with hot boiled potatoes. The fish will keep for 1
week in refrigerator.

60

Crayfish Stromming
Kräftströmming

---

³/₄ kg (1 lb. 10 oz.) whole stromming or
1 to 2 packages frozen fillets of stromming
2 to 3 teaspoons salt
one ¼-can peeled tomatoes
2 teaspoons dill seed or 4 to 5 tablespoons finely chopped dill

Clean the fish and remove the back bone; rinse well. Defrost the frozen fish. Sprinkle with salt and roll up each fillet, skinside in. Put the rolls close to each other in a wide shallow casserole. Pour in the tomatoes with their liquid. Sprinkle with dill. Bring to a simmer and cook, covered, over low heat for 20 to 30 minutes. Chill well before serving.

Tarragon Stromming
Dragonströmming

---

³/₄ kg (1 lb. 10 oz.) whole stromming
4 dl (1³/₄ cups) water
3 tablespoons Swedish spirit vinegar
1¹/₂ teaspoons salt

DRESSING
1 dl (¹/₂ cup) or 100 g (3¹/₂ oz.) mayonnaise
1 dl (¹/₂ cup) cream-fil, sour cream or whipping cream
¹/₂ to 1 crushed garlic clove
salt, white pepper
1 teaspoon dried tarragon
2 to 3 tablespoons finely chopped parsley

Clean and fillet the stromming. Remove the skin. Stir together the water, vinegar and salt; pour over the fish and refrigerate for 24 hours. Drain well.
Stir the mayonnaise with cream-fil, sour cream or whipped cream. Season to taste with garlic, salt, pepper, tarragon and parsley. Pour the dressing over the fish and chill for about 1 hour. Serve with toasted bread and cool beer.

Fried Stromming
Strömmingsflundror

¾ to 1 kg (1 lb. 10 oz. to
2 lb. 3 oz.) whole
stromming or
1 pkg frozen fillets of
stromming
salt

FILLING
2 tablespoons margarine
or butter
50 g (about 2 oz.) finely
chopped parsley or
3 to 4 tablespoons grated
horseradish
flour, fine dry bread
crumbs
salt, white pepper
margarine, butter or oil

Clean the fish and remove the backbone. Defrost the frozen fish. Stir the margarine or butter with chopped parsley or grated horseradish. Put two fillets together, skinside out, with a little filling between. Dip both sides in flour mixed with bread crumbs, salt and pepper. Heat a skillet with margarine, butter or oil. When the foam subsides, add the fish and fry both sides till a golden brown. Serve at once with mashed or boiled potatoes and creamed vegetables.

Chimney Sweepers
Sotare

¾ to 1 kg (1 lb. 10 oz. to
2 lb. 3 oz.) whole
stromming
1 tablespoon salt

SALT WATER
1 liter (4 cups) water
3 tablespoons salt

GREEN CREAM
1 to 1½ dl (½ to ¾ cup)
light cream
finely chopped chives,
parsley and dill
salt, white pepper

Clean the fish but do not remove the backbone, only the head, tail and intestines. Rinse well and rub with salt. Brush with oil and broil the fish for 3 to 4 minutes in a hot cast iron skillet or inside a rack over open fire. Immerse the fish in the salt water for a second and serve at once with green cream and potatoes boiled in their jackets. Flavor the cream with finely chopped herbs, salt and pepper to taste.

Stromming Casserole
Strömmingslåda

1 kg (2 lb. 3 oz.) whole
stromming
1 tablespoon salt
1 teaspoon 4-spices
1 leek, sliced
5 tablespoons grated
cheese
1 dl (¹/₂ cup) light cream
2 tablespoons margarine
or butter
2 tomatoes, sliced
finely chopped parsley

Clean the fish and remove the backbone. Rinse and drain. Sprinkle with salt and fold each fish so that it looks whole. Place the fish, belly down, in a buttered baking dish. Sprinkle with the spices, then the sliced leek and, finally, the cheese. Pour in the cream and dot with margarine or butter. Add the sliced tomatoes either before or after baking. Bake in a 200° oven for about 30 minutes. Serve hot; sprinkle with chopped parsley before serving.

Buckling in Mustard Marinade
Senapsmarinerad böckling

3 to 4 bucklings (smoked
stromming)
or
1 large smoked herring

MARINADE
2 to 3 tablespoons oil
1 tablespoon red wine
vinegar
1 to 2 tablespoons
prepared mustard
white pepper

GARNISH
1 tart apple, diced
1 yellow onion, diced
1 pickled beet, diced
2 tablespoons finely
chopped dill
lemon juice

Clean and fillet the fish. Remove as many small bones as possible. Put the fillets on a serving platter. Beat together the ingredients for the marinade, season it to taste and pour over the fish. Garnish with rows of diced apple, onion, beet, dill and parsley. Press a little lemon juice over the apple to prevent discoloring.

Poached Cod
Kokt torsk

1 kg (2 lb. 3 oz.) whole
cod or
³/₄ kg (1 lb. 10 oz.) cod cut
in thick slices
1¹/₂ to 2 tablespoons salt
2 liter (8 cups) water
1 to 2 slices yellow onion
2 parsley sprigs
1 lemon

Clean and rinse the fish well. In a kettle, combine the salt and water. Put the whole fish in warm water, put fish cut in slices in simmering water. Add the onion and parsley sprigs. Simmer the fish slowly for 10 to 15 minutes. Transfer to serving platter and garnish with parsley and lemon wedges. Serve with boiled potatoes and white sauce flavored with mustard or chopped egg and parsley. Or serve the fish with melted butter and chopped hard-boiled egg.
Pike, pike perch, hake and other fish may be prepared in the same way.

Stewed Haddock
Råstuvad kolja

400 to 500 g (14 oz. to
about 1 lb.) fresh or 1 pkg
frozen fillets of haddock
600 g (1 lb. 5 oz.) potatoes
2 tablespoons finely
chopped parsley
salt, white pepper
2 tablespoons flour or fine
dry bread crumbs
50 g (about 2 oz.)
margarine or butter
3 to 4 dl (1¹/₂ to 1³/₄ cups)
boiling water or fish
bouillon
2 tablespoons pickled
onions
chopped parsley, pimento

Cut the fillets in pieces. If frozen fish is used, defrost it slightly and cut in oblique slices. Peel and slice the potatoes. Put the fish, potatoes, parsley, spices and flour in layers in a casserole that can be brought to the table. Add the margarine or butter, pour in the water or fish bouillon. Bring to a simmer and cook, covered, over low heat on top of the stove, or in a 175° oven, for 20 to 30 minutes or till the potatoes are tender. Garnish with pickled onions, chopped parsley and sliced pimento.

Fried Stromming (p. 62) served with Creamed Potatoes (p. 51).

Basic White Fish Sauce
Grundrecept för varm fisksås

1 to 2 tablespoons margarine or butter
2 to 3 tablespoons flour
3 to 4 dl (1¹/₂ to 1³/₄ cups) fish bouillon and milk or cream
salt, white pepper

In a saucepan, melt the margarine or butter. Stir in the flour and cook for a few minutes. Gradually add the liquid, constantly stirring. Use fish bouillon or milk, or use fish bouillon mixed with milk or cream. Let the sauce cook over medium heat for a few minutes, occasionally stirring. Season to taste with salt and pepper. If desired, flavor the sauce with any of the following. Serve with hot poached fish.

- 4 to 5 finely chopped anchovy fillets
- juice of ¹/₄ to ¹/₂ lemon
- 1 to 3 teaspoons curry powder
- 2 tablespoons finely chopped dill; fresh, frozen or dried
- 2 tablespoons finely chopped chives, leek or parsley
- 1 to 2 tablespoons coarsely chopped capers
- 1 to 2 tablespoons smoked cod roe caviar
- 2 tablespoons finely chopped, sautéed yellow onion
- 100 to 150 g (3¹/₂ to 5 oz.) cooked cleaned shrimps
- 3 to 4 cooked cleaned sea-crayfish, cut in pieces
- 1 to 2 chopped hard-boiled eggs
- 1 to 2 tablespoons grated horseradish
- 1 to 2 tablespoons prepared mustard or 1 teaspoon mustard powder
- 1 to 2 tablespoons mustard seed, finely crushed and mixed with a little water
- one ¹/₄-can sliced mushrooms, drained and sautéed

Glassblower's Herring (p. 56).

Summer Casserole
Sommargryta

6 to 8 perch or whiting
(about 1¹/₂ kg or 3 lb. 5 oz.)
1 tablespoon salt
¹/₂ to 1 dl (¹/₄ to ¹/₂ cup)
finely chopped dill and
chives
2 tablespoons flour
2 to 3 tablespoons
margarine or butter
juice of ¹/₂ to 1 lemon
water
4 tomatoes, cut in wedges

Clean and fillet the fish. Rinse quickly and sprinkle with salt. Put the fish and chopped herbs in layers in a casserole that can be brought to the table. Stir together the flour and margarine or butter to a smooth paste; dot over the fish. Add the lemon juice and enough water to reach the fish halfway up. Let the fish simmer, covered, for a few minutes, then add the tomato wedges. Let simmer for a few minutes more. Serve hot with boiled potatoes and a tossed salad.

Frozen **cod, haddock** and other fish may be prepared in the same way. Thaw the fish slightly and cut in slices.

Pickled Salmon
Inkokt lax

1 kg (2 lb. 3 oz.) fresh
salmon
³/₄ tablespoon salt
1 bay leaf
4 to 5 white peppercorns
a few dill sprigs
2 slices yellow onion
¹/₂ liter (2 cups) warm
water
¹/₂ to 1 dl (¹/₄ to ¹/₂ cup)
swedish table vinegar

Clean and rinse the fish, cut in pieces 3 to 4 cm thick. Put the fish in a low, wide saucepan or fish kettle. Add the spices, dill and onion. Pour in the water mixed with vinegar. Let simmer for 8 to 10 minutes. Transfer the fish to a serving dish and pour the hot stock over. Let cool. Serve with cold mustard sauce or mayonnaise.

Eel, mackerel, lumpfish and **herring** may be prepared in the same way.

Cold Mustard Sauce
Senapsfil

2 dl (about 1 cup) cream-fil or sour cream
1 egg yolk
1½ to 2 teaspoons prepared mustard
salt, white pepper
red wine vinegar

Stir together the cream, egg yolk and mustard. Season to taste with salt, pepper and, if desired, vinegar. Serve with cold poached fish or fish salads.

Variation: Instead of mustard, flavor the sauce with paprika, curry powder or finely chopped dill, chives or parsley.

Gravlax

1 to 1¼ kg (2 lb. 3 oz. to 2 lb. 12 oz.) fresh salmon, center cut
¾ dl (½ cup) salt
½ dl (¼ cup) sugar
20 coarsely crushed white peppercorns
50 g (about 2 oz.) chopped dill

Clean the salmon and cut in fillets. Do not remove the skin. Wipe the fish dry with a paper towel; do not rinse. Rub the fish with the salt mixed with sugar. Sprinkle part of the salt mixture and some dill in a deep enamel or stainless steel baking dish. Place one piece salmon, skinside down, in the dish and sprinkle generously with dill, crushed peppercorns and salt mixture. Cover with the second piece of salmon, skinside up. Sprinkle with the remaining salt mixture. Cover with aluminum foil and a light weight, e.g. a chopping board. Refrigerate for at least 1 to 2 days. Turn the salmon around every day. The gravlax will keep for 1 to 3 weeks in refrigerator.
To serve, cut in slices free from the skin. Sauté the skin in hot skillet, roll it up and use as garnish for the salmon. Garnish, too, with lettuce, dill and lemon wedges. Serve with the following gravlax sauce.

Gravlax Sauce
Gravlaxsås

3 tablespoons oil
1 tablespoon red wine
vinegar
1 tablespoon sugar
$^1/_3$ teaspoon salt
1 pinch white pepper
2 to 3 tablespoons
prepared mustard
2 to 3 tablespoons finely
chopped dill

Shake or beat together all the ingredients except dill. Add the dill or serve it from a separate bowl.

Salmon Pudding
Laxpudding

200 g (7 oz.) salt salmon
$^3/_4$ kg (1 lb. 10 oz.)
potatoes
3 tablespoons chopped
dill
white pepper
4 eggs
4 dl (1$^3/_4$ cups) milk

Soak the fish in cold water overnight, about 12 hours. Wipe it dry and cut in pieces. Peel and slice the potatoes. Put the potatoes and salmon in layers in a buttered baking dish. Sprinkle with dill and a little pepper between the layers. The first and last layer should be potatoes. Beat together the eggs and milk, pour into the baking dish. Bake in a 175° oven for about 1 hour. Serve with melted butter.

Smoked Warm Salmon Trout
Rökt varm laxöring

1 to 1$^1/_4$ kg (2 lb. 3 oz. to
2 lb. 11$^1/_2$ oz.) smoked
salmon trout
lettuce
dill
radishes
lemon

Wrap the fish with aluminum foil and place on a rack. Heat in a 200° oven for 25 to 30 minutes or until thoroughly hot.
If desired, decorate the fish by making slits in the skin before putting it in the oven; after heating, pull off part of the skin. Put the fish on a heated platter and garnish with lettuce, radishes, dill and lemon wedges. Serve with boiled new potatoes and horseradish cream, that is, whipped cream seasoned with grated horseradish, salt, vinegar and pepper to taste.

Gravlax (p. 67) with Gravlax sauce.

Broiled Perch
Halstrad abborre

1 to 1¹/₄ kg (2 lb. 3 oz. to
2 lb. 11¹/₂ oz.) perch
oil

Broil the perch whole or in fillets, as desired. When broiled whole, the fish need not be scaled, just cleaned. Brush with oil and broil for 8 to 10 minutes over a grill, in a rack over open fire or in hot ungreased cast iron skillet. Remove the skin and serve with salt and butter flavored with lemon juice.

Whitefish, whiting, herring and **trout** may be prepared in the same way.

Fried Plaice with Capers and Beets
Stekt rödspättefilé med kapris och rödbeta

500 g (about 1 lb.) fresh
or 1 pkg frozen fillets
of plaice
1 egg white, lightly beaten
2 tablespoons fine dry
bread crumbs
2 tablespoons flour
¹/₂ to ³/₄ tablespoon salt
75 g (2¹/₄ oz.) margarine
or butter

GARNISH
2 tablespoons capers
3 tablespoons finely
chopped pickled beets
1 tablespoon finely
chopped parsley

If frozen fish is used, defrost for 30 minutes and cut in oblique 1 cm thick slices. Dip the fish in the beaten egg white, then in the flour mixed with bread crumbs and salt. Heat a skillet with part of the margarine or butter. When the foam subsides, add the fish and fry till a golden brown. Remove to heated serving platter. Brown the remaining margarine or butter; stir in the capers, beets and parsley. Heat and pour over the fish. Serve with boiled potatoes.

Most kinds of fish, e.g. **cod, haddock, mackerel** and **herring,** may be prepared in the same way.

70

Fried Mackerel with Dill Sauce
Stekt makrill med dillsky

1 kg (2 lb. 3 oz.) mackerel
2 tablespoons flour
2 tablespoons fine dry
bread crumbs
salt, white pepper
margarine or butter
$^1/_2$ dl ($^1/_4$ cup) finely
chopped dill
water

Clean and fillet the fish. Rinse well and wipe the fillets dry. Dip in the flour mixed with bread crumbs, salt and pepper. Heat a skillet with a little margarine or butter. When the foam subsides, add the fish and fry until nicely browned on both sides. Add the dill and a little water; let cook over low heat for a few minutes. Serve with boiled potatoes and tomato salad.

Ovenbaked Fillets of Whitefish
Ugnsstekt sikfilé

1 kg (2 lb. 3 oz.) whitefish
$^3/_4$ tablespoon salt
1 tablespoon finely
chopped yellow onion
2 to 3 tablespoons
margarine or butter
100 g (3$^1/_2$ oz.) fresh
mushrooms or
one $^1/_8$-can mushrooms
1 dl ($^1/_2$ cup) crumbed
white bread
1 to 2 tablespoons finely
chopped parsley

Clean and fillet the fish. Rub with salt. Sauté the onion in the margarine or butter. Trim and slice or chop the mushrooms; let cook along with the onion. Pour into a buttered baking dish and mix in the bread crumbs and parsley. Place the fish on top. Bake in a 200 to 225° oven for 10 to 15 minutes. Baste the fish often; add a little water if necessary. For extra fine taste, add 1 to 2 tablespoons white vermouth. Serve the fish directly from the baking dish. Bake whole fish in the same way; allow 20 to 25 minutes cooking time.
Carp, grayling, pike, pike perch and **whitefish** may be prepared in the same way.

Ovenbaked Pike
Ugnsstekt gädda

1 kg (2 lb. 3 oz.) pike
lemon juice
1 egg white, lightly beaten
2 tablespoons flour
1/2 tablespoon salt
2 tablespoons fine dry
bread crumbs
50 g (about 2 oz.)
margarine or butter
1 small yellow onion,
finely chopped
2 to 3 dl (about 1 to 1 1/2
cups) light cream

Clean and rinse the fish. Sprinkle with a little fresh lemon juice. Brush with beaten egg white and dip the fish in the flour mixed with salt and bread crumbs. Place the fish in a buttered baking dish and sprinkle with chopped onion; dot with margarine or butter. Bake in a 200 to 225° oven for 25 to 30 minutes. Baste the fish now and then. When it begins to brown, add the cream and continue basting. **Cod, whitefish, eel** and other fish may be prepared in the same way.

Ovenbaked Lutfisk
Lutfisk kokt i ugn

1 1/2 kg (3 lb. 5 oz.) lutfisk
1 tablespoon salt

Place the fish, skinside down, in a buttered deep baking dish. Or, if desired, first remove the skin. (Frozen fish may be cooked in its wrapping.) Sprinkle the fish with salt and cover the dish with aluminum foil. Cook in a 200° oven for 30 to 40 minutes. Pour off the liquid and serve the fish hot with boiled potatoes, peas, mustard sauce or white sauce, melted butter and allspice or white pepper.

White Lutfisk Sauce
Vit sås

50 g (2 oz.) margarine
or butter
3 tablespoons flour
3 to 4 dl (1 1/2 to 1 3/4 cups)
milk
1 teaspoon salt
white pepper

In a saucepan, melt the margarine or butter. Stir in the flour and gradually add the milk. Beat the sauce until smooth and let cook for a few minutes. Season to taste with salt and pepper. Serve with coarsely crushed allspice and black pepper.

Mustard Sauce
Skånsk senapssås

**1 recipe white lutfisk
sauce
1 tablespoon dark
mustard seed
1 to 2 tablespoons water
or
1 to 2 tablespoons
prepared Skåne mustard**

Pound the mustard seed with mortar and pestle or use the special mustard ball. Mix with the water and stir into the white sauce. Or flavor the sauce with prepared mustard.

MEAT
AND
POULTRY

The two most common meats in Sweden are beef and pork, but veal and lamb are much used, too. The traditional Swedish Sunday dinner of veal pot roast with light cream sauce, pickled cucumber and red currant jelly is today often replaced by a fried chicken or chicken casserole, food that formerly was reserved for very special occasions only. Reindeer meat from Lapland is available all over the country; the dark lean meat has a flavor similar to venison.

Beef Patties with Onions
Pannbiff med lök

2 cold boiled potatoes
400 g (14 oz.) ground beef
salt, white pepper
1 to 2 dl light cream
and water
2 to 4 large yellow
onions, sliced
2 tablespoons margarine
or butter

Mash the potatoes and mix with the meat. Add salt, pepper, cream and water. Work the meat mixture smooth and shape to patties. Heat a skillet with part of the margarine or butter. When the foam subsides, add the onions and cook over moderate heat until golden brown. Transfer the onions to a platter and keep hot.

Heat the remaining margarine or butter in the skillet and fry the patties over moderate heat until brown on both sides. Remove the patties to a heated serving platter and spread the onions on top. Add a little water to the skillet, heat and stir. Serve the patties with the pan juices, boiled or fried potatoes and vegetables.

Beef Patties à la Lindström
Biff à la Lindström

Follow the recipe for Beef Patties with Onions but add 2 finely chopped small pickled beets, 2 tablespoons finely chopped yellow onion and 2 tablespoons capers to the meat mixture.

Cabbage Rolls
Kåldolmar

1 small head white
cabbage
water, salt

FILLING
1 dl (¹/₂ cup) water
¹/₂ dl (¹/₄ cup) regular
white rice
3 dl (1¹/₂ cups) milk
350 g (about 12 oz.)
ground beef
salt, white pepper
thyme
margarine or butter
1 dl (¹/₂ cup) light cream

Cut out part of the core and put the cabbage in salted boiling water. Cook, covered, till the leaves are slightly soft and easy to remove from the core. Peel off the leaves one by one and drain on a rack or towel. Trim the coarse center vein of each leaf.
To make the filling, bring the water to a boil. Add the rice and cook, covered, until the water is almost absorbed. Stir in the milk and cook till the mixture resembles a thin porridge. Let cool. Mix with the meat and spices, add more milk if necessary. Put a large tablespoonful of filling on each cabbage leaf. Fold the leaf around the filling and secure the roll with a toothpick.
Heat a skillet with a little margarine or butter. When the foam subsides, add a few rolls and brown them well all around over moderate heat. Transfer to a casserole. When all the cabbage rolls are browned, add a little beef bouillon or water to the casserole, cover and let simmer for about 30 minutes. Add the cream and cook for another 15 minutes. Serve with boiled potatoes and lingonberry preserve.

Meatballs
Köttbullar

1 dl (½ cup) fine dry
bread crumbs
1 dl (½ cup) light cream
1 dl (½ cup) water
200 g (7 oz.) ground beef
200 g (7 oz.) ground
lean pork
1½ teaspoons salt
½ teaspoon ground
allspice
2 tablespoons grated
yellow onion
(or 1 to 2 crushed
garlic cloves)
1 egg, beaten
3 tablespoons margarine
or butter

Mix the bread crumbs, cream and water; set aside for 5 minutes. Work together the beef, pork, salt, allspice and onion. Gradually add the bread crumbs, then the egg. Blend well and fry a sample to test the seasoning.

Shape into balls. Make large meatballs to be served for dinner or small meatballs for the smörgåsbord. Heat part of the margarine or butter in a skillet. When the foam subsides, add 10 to 15 meatballs. Cook over moderate heat until the meatballs are beautifully brown and cooked through. Transfer to a serving dish and keep hot while cooking the remaining meatballs. Serve with boiled potatoes, lingonberry preserve and a tossed salad.

Swedish Hash
Pytt i panna

3 tablespoons margarine
or butter
8 to 10 potatoes, peeled
and cut in small cubes
2 yellow onions, finely
chopped
100 g (3½ oz.) smoked
ham, cut in small cubes
4 dl (1¾ cups) boiled or
roast beef, cut in small
cubes
1 teaspoon salt
white pepper
finely chopped parsley
4 egg yolks

Heat a skillet with part of the margarine or butter. When the foam subsides, add the raw potato cubes and cook over moderate heat till golden brown and tender. Remove to a platter. Add the remaining margarine or butter to the skillet and cook the onions till soft and translucent; mix with the potatoes. Sauté the ham, add the beef and brown it lightly. Return the potatoes and onion to the skillet, mix well. Add salt and pepper to taste, heat the hash thoroughly and transfer to a heated platter. Sprinkle with chopped parsley. Let the egg yolks remain in the half shells and press into the hash; every diner stirs an egg yolk into his serving of hash.

Boiled Falu Sausage with Horseradish Sauce
Kokt falukorv med pepparrotssås

**500 g (about 1 lb.)
falu sausage**
5 dl (2 cups) water
1 to 2 beef bouillon cubes
1 to 2 slices yellow onion
parsley sprig

SAUCE
**2 tablespoons margarine
or butter**
3 to 4 tablespoons flour
3 dl (1$^{1}/_2$ cups) milk
**$^{1}/_2$ to 1 dl ($^{1}/_4$ to $^{1}/_2$ cup)
liquid from cooking the
sausage**
grated horseradish
salt, white pepper

Pull the skin off the sausage and place in a kettle. Add the water, bouillon cubes, onion and parsley. Let simmer, covered, till the sausage is thoroughly hot.
In a small saucepan, melt the margarine or butter. Blend in the flour, then add the milk and cooking liquid. Bring to a boil, beating the sauce until smooth. Let the sauce simmer for a few minutes and season to taste with grated horseradish, salt and pepper. Serve the sausage with the sauce, boiled potatoes and a tossed salad.

Boiled Pork Sausage
Kokt fläskkorv

**about 800 g (about 1 lb.
12 oz.) pork sausage**
4 to 5 whole allspice
$^{1}/_2$ to 1 bay leaf
water

Rinse the sausage and put in a wide saucepan. Add the spices and enough water to cover the sausage. Let simmer, uncovered, for 30 minutes. Carefully turn the sausage around once during this time. Cut in thick slices and serve with mashed potatoes or rutabagas (swedes). Or serve with boiled potatoes and white sauce flavored with mustard, horseradish or parsley.
The same recipe may be used for **köttkorv** or meat sausage, **Värmland sausage** and **grynkorv**. Cook the latter two for 45 minutes.

Spare Ribs
Revbensspjäll

1 kg (2 lb. 3 oz.) spare ribs

SEASONINGS
1 teaspoon salt
1 teaspoon ginger
1 pinch white pepper

or

2 dl (about 1 cup)
chili sauce
1/2 dl (1/4 cup) finely
chopped yellow onion
2 crushed garlic cloves
juice of 1/2 orange
2 tablespoons red wine
vinegar
2 tablespoons oil
1 teaspoon prepared
mustard
1/2 teaspoon salt
1/2 teaspoon freshly
ground white pepper
1 teaspoon Worchester-
shire sauce

Rub the meat with any of the two spice mixtures. Or beat together the ingredients for the second spice mixture and brush the meat. Place it on a rotating spit or put the meat, fat side up, on a rack in a shallow roasting pan. Broil for 1 to 1 1/2 hours. Or roast for about 1 1/2 hours in a 175° oven; turn the meat around once.

Dilute the pan drippings with a little water, add salt and pepper to taste. If desired, make a gravy by adding 2 tablespoons flour stirred with a little water to a smooth paste. Let the sauce cook for a few minutes. Cut the meat in serving pieces and serve with the pan juices or sauce, boiled potatoes, apple sauce and, if desired, brussels sprouts or red cabbage.

Pork Sauce from Småland
Smålandsdoppa

200 g (7 oz.) lightly salted
side pork
1 small yellow onion,
finely chopped
3 tablespoons flour
5 dl (2 cups) milk
salt, white pepper

Cut the pork in small cubes. Heat a skillet and brown the pork without adding margarine or butter. Add the chopped onion and cook for a few minutes together with the pork. Sprinkle with the flour and gradually add the milk. Let the sauce cook for a few minutes and season to taste with salt and pepper. Serve with potatoes boiled in their jackets.

Fried Pork with Onion Sauce
Stekt fläsk med löksås

400 g (14 oz.) lightly salted side pork
1 large yellow onion, finely chopped
2 tablespoons flour
4 dl (1³/₄ cups) milk
salt, white pepper

Cut the pork in slices and fry in hot skillet without adding margarine or butter; cook for 2 to 3 minutes on each side depending on how crisp you like your pork. Transfer to a platter and keep hot.

Sauté the chopped onion in the fat remaining in the skillet. Stir in the flour and then the milk. Blend well and let the sauce cook for a few minutes, it should be quite thick. Add salt and pepper to taste. Serve the pork with the sauce, boiled potatoes and vegetables.

Hunter's Pork
Jägarfläsk

2 large slices fresh pork shoulder (together about 500 g or 1 lb.)
1 tablespoon prepared mustard
2 apples, cut in wedges
12 prunes, pitted
salt, white pepper
2 tablespoons margarine or butter
6 small yellow onions, peeled
1 medium carrot, sliced
beef bouillon or water
parsley sprigs

Remove the rind and flatten the pork. Place the two slices side by side, one slightly overlapping the other. Spread with mustard. Arrange the apples and prunes in rows on top. Sprinkle with salt and pepper. Roll up the pork to a thick roll, secure it with toothpicks. Heat the margarine or butter in a heavy kettle. When the foam subsides, add the pork roll and brown it well on all sides. Add the onions and carrot slices, let brown lightly. Pour in a little beef bouillon or water and add a few parsley sprigs. Cover and let simmer for about 1 hour. Baste the roll now and then. Add more bouillon as needed. Slice the roll and serve with raw-fried potatoes, a tossed salad and pan juices.

Swedish Beef Stew
Kalops

1 kg (2 lb. 3 oz.) beef with bones or
600 g (1 lb. 5 oz.) boneless beef: rib, rump, brisket or bottom round
3 tablespoons margarine or butter
3 tablespoons flour
1½ teaspoons salt
2 yellow onions, sliced
1 bay leaf
10 whole allspice
4 to 5 dl (1¾ to 2 cups) water

Cut the meat in large cubes. Heat the margarine or butter in a heavy kettle. When the foam subsides, add the meat and brown it well on all sides. Sprinkle with the flour and salt, stir the meat. Add the onions, bay leaf, allspice and water. Cover and simmer till tender, 1½ to 2 hours. Serve with boiled potatoes, pickled beets and tossed salad.

Variation: When the meat has cooked 1 hour, add 2 sliced carrots and 2 leeks cut in pieces. The stew may also be prepared with elk or reindeer meat. Prepare veal stew the same way but use half the allspice and bay leaf.

Swedish Steak with Onions
Svensk biff med lök

3 tablespoons margarine or butter
4 large yellow onions, sliced
4 slices sirloin or top round of beef (about 55 g or 1 lb.)
salt, white pepper

Heat a skillet with part of the margarine or butter. When the foam subsides, add the onions. Lower the heat and cook until the onions are golden brown and tender. Remove to a platter and keep hot.
Pound the meat lightly with the back of your hand. Heat the remaining margarine or butter in the skillet and fry the steaks for about 3 minutes on each side. Season with salt and pepper and remove the steaks to a heated serving platter. Spread the fried onions on top. Add a little water to the skillet, heat and stir. Serve the steaks at once with the pan juices, boiled, baked or fried potatoes and tossed salad.

A Christmas Table with crispbread, fruit, a leg of mutton and the indispensable Christmas Ham (p. 87).

Beef Roulades
Oxrulader

8 slices (about 600 g or
about 1 lb.) boneless beef:
sirloin or top round
1 teaspoon salt
white pepper

FILLING
8 Swedish anchovy
fillets
2 tablespoons finely
chopped yellow onion
2 tablespoons margarine
or butter
1 dl (¹/₂ cup) water

Sprinkle the meat with salt and pepper. Put one anchovy fillet and a little chopped onion on each slice and roll it up. Secure the roulades with toothpicks.

Heat a skillet with the margarine or butter. When the foam subsides, add the roulades and brown them well on all sides. Add the water and cover. Simmer for about 1 hour or till tender. If desired, then remove the roulades and make a sauce by adding flour stirred with a little cream to a smooth paste. Let the sauce cook for a few minutes and return the roulades.

Serve the roulades with the pan juices or sauce, boiled or fried potatoes, vegetables, lingonberry preserve and cucumber salad.

Sailor's Beef
Sjömansbiff

400 to 500 g (14 oz. to
about 1 lb.) boneless beef:
rib, rump or top round
3 tablespoons margarine
or butter
1¹/₂ teaspoons salt
white pepper
2 large yellow onions,
sliced
10 to 12 potatoes, peeled
and sliced
3 dl (1¹/₂ cups) water
or beer

Cut the meat in slices. Heat a skillet with part of the margarine or butter. When the foam subsides, add the meat and brown on both sides. Season with salt and pepper. Brown the onions in the remaining margarine or butter. Put the meat, onions and potatoes in layers in an oven-to-table casserole; the first and last layer should be potatoes. Sprinkle a little salt on the potatoes. Add water or beer, cover and let simmer for about 45 minutes.

Fried Pork with Onion sauce (p. 79), served with potatoes boiled in their jackets.

Veal in Dill Sauce
Dillkött

1 kg (2 lb. 3 oz.) breast
of veal
2 teaspoons salt
1 liter (4 cups) water
10 white peppercorns
3 cloves
1 bay leaf
1 carrot, sliced
1 yellow onion
dill sprigs

SAUCE
2 tablespoons margarine
or butter
3 tablespoons flour
3 dl (1$^{1}/_{2}$ cups) liquid
from cooking the veal
1 dl ($^{1}/_{2}$ cup) light cream
+ 1 egg yolk
salt, white pepper
finely chopped dill
fresh lemon juice

Put the meat in a kettle, add the salt and enough water to cover. Bring to a boil. Remove the scum on the surface and lower the heat. Add the spices, cover and simmer for 1 hour. Then add the carrot, onion and dill sprigs. Let simmer for another 20 minutes. Remove the meat, cut in serving pieces and keep hot. Strain the cooking liquid.

In a small saucepan, melt the margarine or butter. Blend in the flour. Add the cooking liquid and bring to a boil, beating the sauce until smooth. Let cook for a few minutes. Remove from heat and beat in the cream mixed with the egg yolk. Season the sauce with salt, pepper, dill and lemon juice. Pour it over the meat or serve it separately. Serve with boiled potatoes or rice.

Instead of veal, pork shanks cut in slices may be used. When cooked, remove the fat and rind.

Roast Lamb
Lammstek

1 kg (2 lb. 3 oz.)
lamb roast
1$^{1}/_{2}$ teaspoons salt
white pepper
1 garlic clove
parsley sprig

SAUCE
4 dl (1$^{3}/_{4}$ cups) pan juices
2 tablespoons flour
cream

Place the roast, fat side up, on a rack in a roasting pan. Rub with salt and pepper. Insert the garlic clove and parsley sprig close to the bone. Roast in a 175° oven for little less than 2 hours. When a meat thermometer is used, roast until it reads 82°. Allow the roast to rest on top of the stove for 10 minutes before carving.

Dilute the pan juices with hot water to make 4 dl. Bring to a boil. Stir in the flour mixed with a little cream to a smooth paste. Beat until smooth and let the sauce cook for a few minutes. Season to taste with salt and white pepper.

82

Pot Roast
Grytstek

**2 tablespoons margarine
or butter
1 kg (2 lb. 3 oz.) rump or
top round of beef, elk,
reindeer, veal or pork
1¹/₂ to 2 teaspoons salt
white or black pepper
1 bay leaf**

SAUCE
**4 dl (1³/₄ cups) pan juices
mixed with cream
2 tablespoons flour
salt, white pepper**

Heat the margarine or butter in a heavy kettle. When the foam subsides, add the meat and brown it well all around. Season with salt and pepper. Add the bay leaf and a little hot water, cover and let the roast cook over low heat: 1¹/₂ to 2 hours for beef, elk and reindeer, 1 hour for pork and veal. Baste the roast now and then, adding more water as needed. Remove the roast and allow to rest for 10 minutes before carving. Mix the pan juices with cream to make 4 dl. Add the flour stirred with a little cream to a smooth paste. Bring to a boil, beating the sauce until smooth. Let cook for a few minutes. Season the sauce with salt and pepper to taste. Serve the roast with the sauce, boiled potatoes, vegetables, red currant jelly and pickles.

Game Casserole with Red Wine
Viltgryta med rödvin

**400 g (14 oz.) boneless
meat of elk, venison or
reindeer
2 tablespoons flour
1 teaspoon salt
white pepper
3 tablespoons margarine
or butter
2 carrots, sliced
1 yellow onion, chopped
3 to 4 dl (1¹/₂ to 1³/₄ cups)
red wine**

Cut the meat in cubes and dip in flour mixed with salt and pepper. Heat a skillet with the margarine or butter. When the foaam subsides, add the meat and cook until browned on all sides. Add the carrots, onion and wine. Simmer, covered, till the meat is tender. Serve with rice and a green salad.

Reindeer Casserole
Renskavpanna

1 pkg frozen sliced
reindeer meat
2 tablespoons margarine
or butter
2 yellow onions, finely
chopped
1 teaspoon salt
white or black pepper
1 to 2 dl (½ to about
1 cup) light cream
1 to 2 teaspoons
prepared mustard
finely chopped parsley

Heat a skillet with the margarine or butter. When the foam subsides, add the frozen meat. Gradually separate the meat slices as they cook. Fry until nicely browned. Add the chopped onions and cook together with the meat for a few minutes. Season with salt and pepper, then stir in the cream and mustard. Simmer for a few minutes. Sprinkle with chopped parsley and serve hot with boiled potatoes and vegetables.

Roast Saddle of Reindeer
Rensadel

5 to 6 servings

1 saddle of reindeer, about
1½ kg (3 lb. 5 oz.)
2 teaspoons salt
white pepper

SAUCE
3½ dl (about 1½ cups)
pan drippings mixed with
beef bouillon
2 tablespoons flour
½ dl (¼ cup) light cream
salt, white pepper
blue cheese
red currant jelly

If frozen, defrost the saddle so that the membranes and small silvery sinews can be removed. Rub with salt and pepper, then place the saddle on a rack in a roasting pan. Roast in a 175° oven for 1½ to 2 hours. When a meat thermometer is used, roast till it reads 77°. Allow the roast to rest on top of the stove for 10 minutes. Loosen the meat, carve in slices and put back on the saddle.

Add a little hot water to the roasting pan and stir to dissolve the pan drippings. Mix with beef bouillon to make 3½ dl (1½ cup). Bring to a boil in a small saucepan and stir in the flour mixed with the cream to a smooth paste. Let the sauce cook for a few minutes, beating until smooth. Season to taste with salt, pepper, blue cheese and red currant jelly.

Put the saddle on a serving platter and surround it with green beans and chestnut purée or tomato halves filled with pickled onions. **Saddle of venison** may be cooked and served in the same way.

84

Saddle of Venison served with onions, green beans and
peeled tomatoes is a festive dinner fare.

Roast Goose
Stekt gås

8 to 10 servings

1 goose (about 5 kg or 11 lb.)
1 lemon, cut in wedges
salt, white pepper
(ginger)

STUFFING
4 apples, peeled and cut in half
200 g (7 oz.) prunes

Remove the intestines and rinse well. Pull out the large sinews from the legs of the goose. Rub it inside and out with lemon, salt, white pepper and, if desired, ginger. Stuff the goose with apples and prunes, truss and place it, breast up, on a rack in a shallow roasting pan. Roast in a 175° oven for 2½ to 3 hours. Test the goose by piercing the thigh with a toothpick; if the juice that runs out is clear and colorless, the goose is done. For a nice crisp skin, baste the goose with a few tablespoons cold water and set the oven door ajar the last 15 minutes of roasting time.

Pour the pan drippings into a saucepan and skim off most of the fat. Add a little water to the roasting pan and scrape to dissolve any browned bits sticking to the bottom; mix this with the pan drippings. Bring to a boil and, if desired, make a gravy by adding a little flour or arrowroot. Scoop out the filling and discard. Loosen the legs. Carve the breast meat in oblique slices and put back on the goose so that it looks whole. Serve with boiled potatoes, red cabbage, stewed prunes and apple halves. The apples may be filled with orange mandarins and raisins that have been marinated in vinegar dressing.

Fried Chicken
Stekt broiler

1 broiler chicken
50 g (about 2 oz.) margarine or butter
2 to 3 teaspoons curry powder or paprika
½ to 1 teaspoon salt

If frozen, defrost the chicken. Cut in half or in serving pieces. Melt the margarine or butter in a skillet, stir in the curry powder or paprika. When the foam subsides, add the chicken and fry until nicely browned all around. Sprinkle with salt. Cover and cook over low heat on top of the stove or in a 175° oven for 30 minutes. Serve the chicken hot or cold with a tossed salad.

Chicken Casserole with Mushrooms
Broilergryta med champinjoner

1 broiler chicken
200 g (7 oz.) fresh
mushrooms or
one ¼-can mushrooms
margarine or butter
1½ to 2 tablespoons flour
1½ teaspoons salt
white or black pepper
2½ to 3 dl (1¼ to 1½
cups) chicken or beef
bouillon
1 pkg frozen green beans

If frozen, defrost the chicken. Cut in serving pieces. Trim and slice the fresh mushrooms; drain the canned mushrooms. Heat a skillet with a little margarine or butter and sauté the mushrooms. Transfer to a casserole.

Dip the chicken into the flour mixed with salt and pepper. Heat the skillet adding a little more margarine or butter. When the foam subsides, add the chicken and brown well on all sides. Remove the chicken to the casserole and pour in the bouillon. Cover and let simmer for 10 minutes. Add the beans and cook for another 10 minutes.

Ovenbaked Christmas Ham
Ugnsbakad julskinka

5 to 6 kg (11 lb. to 13 lb.)
lightly salted ham

GLAZE
1 egg yolk
½ tablespoon sugar
2 to 3 tablespoons
prepared mustard
2 to 3 tablespoons fine
dry bread crumbs

Place the ham, rind up, on a rack in a roasting pan lined with aluminum foil. Insert a meat thermometer into the thickest part of the ham. Bake in a 125° oven for 5 to 6 hours or till the thermometer reads 77°. Remove the rind and spread the top of the ham with the egg yolk, sugar and mustard stirred together. Sprinkle with bread crumbs. Bake in a 225° oven until golden brown. Garnish the ham with kale, prunes and an apple or orange. Serve cold cut in thin slices.

The ham may be baked wrapped in aluminum foil; then use a 175° oven. Lightly smoked ham may be prepared in the same way.

Liver Pâté
Leverpastej

Makes 1,4 kg or 3 lb. 1 oz.

**500 g (about 1 lb.)
pork fat
500 g (about 1 lb.)
pork liver
4 anchovy fillets
1 small yellow onion,
finely chopped
50 g (about 2 oz.)
margarine or butter
$^1/_4$ teaspoon white pepper
$^1/_2$ teaspoon salt
1 to 2 tablespoons
potato flour
3 eggs
4 dl ($1^3/_4$ cups) light
cream**

Cut part of the fat in thin slices and line the bottom of a large loaf pan. Grease the sides.
Grind the liver, remaining fat and anchovies twice on meat grinder. Sauté the chopped onion in the margarine or butter. Let cool and add to the liver batter together with the spices. Work in the flour and eggs. Gradually add the cream and work the batter till smooth and well blended. Pour a sample into a small tart pan and cook in saucepan with boiling water. If too soft, add more flour; if to firm, add more cream to the liver batter.
Fill the loaf pan to $^3/_4$ with the batter, cover with aluminum foil or greaseproof paper. Put the pan in a larger pan filled with hot water. Bake in a 200 to 225° oven for $1^1/_2$ hours. If two smaller pans are used, bake for 1 hour only. Let the pâté cool before unmolding.

Pork Sausage
Fläskkorv

Makes about 5 kg or 11 lb.

**3 kg (about 7 lb.) lean pork
1 kg (2 lb. 3 oz.) pork fat
$1^1/_2$ dl ($^3/_4$ cup) potato flour
$2^1/_2$ tablespoons salt
1 tablespoon sugar
$^1/_2$ tablespoon white
pepper
$^1/_2$ tablespoon ginger
$1^1/_2$ to 2 liter (6 to 8 cups)
water or pork bouillon**

SALT MIXTURE
**2 dl (about 1 cup) salt
1 dl (about $^1/_2$ cup) sugar
2 tablespoons saltpeter**

Grind the pork and fat twice on meat grinder. Stir in the flour and spices. Work the batter well, gradually adding the liquid. Fill sausage casings loosely with the batter. Rub with the salt mixture. Store in freezer or brine.

PANCAKES
AND
WAFFLES

Swedish pancakes come in two sizes: there are the large thin pancakes or **tunnpannkakor** baked on a griddle and the small **plättar** cooked in the special **plättpanna,** a cast iron pan with seven shallow depressions. Made from the same kind of batter they are both favorite desserts of the Swedes. They are also an integral part of the traditional Thursday supper which includes pea soup followed by pancakes and blueberry, raspberry, lingonberry or cloudberry preserve.

Swedish Pancakes
Plättar och pannkakor

6 servings

1 dl (¹/₂ cup) flour
3 dl (1¹/₂ cups) rich
milk or
1¹/₂ dl (³/₄ cup) water and
1¹/₂ dl whipping cream
3 eggs
1 pinch salt
3 tablespoons melted
margarine or butter

Beat together the flour and half of the milk, or the water, to a smooth batter. Add the eggs, remaining milk, or cream, salt and melted margarine or butter. Beat until well blended.

To make small pancakes or **plättar,** heat a **plätt-panna** with a little margarine or butter in each depression. When hot, add about 1 tablespoon batter to each section and cook over medium-high heat for 1 minute or till the surface has set and the bottom is a golden brown. Use a small spatula and turn the pancakes around; cook the other side for about half a minute. If possible, serve the pancakes at once. Continue cooking without adding more margarine or butter to the pan. Stir the batter now and then.

To make the larger pancakes, heat a griddle with a

little margarine or butter. Remove from heat, add a few tablespoons batter and tilt the pan to make the batter spread in a thin layer. Cook over medium-high heat for 1 to 2 minutes, then use a long narrow spatula and turn the pancake around. Cook the other side for about half a minute. Serve the pancakes at once, or stack them on a plate and keep hot over a pan with boiling water. If desired, make a pancake **tårta** by stacking the pancakes with apple sauce or other fruit preserve between the layers. Let cool and spread the top with whipped cream. Serve cut in wedges.

Crêpes

Makes about 12 crêpes

2 eggs
3/4 dl (1/2 cup) flour
3 dl (1 1/2 cups) light cream
1/2 teaspoon salt
2 tablespoons melted
margarine or butter
(2 tablespoons grated
cheese)

CREAMED SHELLFISH
2 tablespoons margarine
or butter
4 tablespoons flour
4 dl (1 3/4 cups) liquid
(cream mixed with milk
or liquid from the canned
shellfish)
1/2 to 1 teaspoon salt
white pepper
1 can lobster, crab or
clams (100 g or 3 1/2 oz.)
1 pkg frozen shrimps
(200 g or 7 oz.)

Beat together the eggs, flour and half of the cream to a smooth batter. Add the remaining cream, salt, and melted margarine or butter. Heat a crêpe pan with a little margarine or butter. When hot, remove from heat and add about 2 tablespoons batter. Tilt the pan to make the batter spread in a thin layer. Cook over medium-high heat for about 1 minute, then remove the crêpe. Stir the batter now and then.
Put a string of creamed shellfish on the unbaked side of each crêpe and roll it up. Serve at once. Or serve the crêpes au gratin: put the rolls in a buttered baking dish and sprinkle with the cheese. Bake in a 250° oven until the cheese is a golden brown.
To make the creamed shellfish, melt the margarine or butter in a saucepan. Stir in the flour. Add the liquid and bring to a boil, beating until smooth. Let cook for 3 to 5 minutes. Season to taste with salt and pepper. Remove from heat and fold in the shellfish.

Variation: Instead of shellfish, mushrooms, asparagus or sweetbread may be used for the filling.

Swedish Pancakes (p. 89) may be served with fresh fruit or
fruit preserve or, as in this case, with icecream.

Thin Pancakes with Pork
Tunna fläskpannkakor

2 eggs
3 dl (1¹/₂ cups) flour
6 dl (about 3 cups) milk
(¹/₂ teaspoon salt)
200 g (7 oz.) lightly salted
lean side pork

Beat together the eggs, flour and half of the milk to a smooth batter. Add the remaining milk and, if desired, salt. Cut the pork in small cubes; cook in hot skillet until brown and mix with the pancake batter. Heat a pancake griddle with a little margarine or butter. Add enough batter to cover the griddle in a thin layer. Cook over moderate heat for a couple of minutes or till set on the surface, then turn the pancake around. Cook the other side for about 1 minute. Try to get the same amount of pork in each pancake. Serve hot with lingonberry preserve.

Crisp Waffles
Frasvåfflor

Makes 6 to 8 large waffles

2¹/₂ dl (1¹/₄ cups) flour
1¹/₂ dl (³/₄ cup) cold water
2¹/₂ dl (1¹/₄ cups)
whipping cream

Beat together the flour and water. When smooth, add about ¹/₂ dl (¹/₄ cup) cream. Whip the remaining cream until thick and fold into the batter. Heat the waffle iron; do not grease. Cook each waffle until crisp and golden brown. Serve the waffles instantly as they come off the iron. Never stack them; if the waffles must wait, spread them on wire rack. Serve with strawberry, raspberry or cloudberry preserve and whipped cream or vanilla ice cream.

PASTRIES
AND
DESSERTS

The traditional Swedish coffee table used to include a sweet yeast bread, one or two plain cakes, numerous cookies and a fancy filled cake called **tårta**. Still a common form of entertaining, the coffee party today is a much less elaborate affair that may feature just one or two baked items, maybe the popular **sockerkaka** and a few cookies. On festive occasions, such as birthdays and namedays, a tårta is a must.

Fresh fruit and ice cream are maybe the two most common desserts in Sweden. Swedish apples are delicious and so are the pears, red and black currants, gooseberries and strawberries grown in the country. Among the wild berries, of prime importance are lingonberries, blueberries and cloudberries.

The cloudberry, an exquisite fruit from the marshes of northern Sweden, looks somewhat like a yellow raspberry but has a distinctive delightful flavor of its own. Vanilla ice cream with a topping of fresh or frozen cloudberries, or cloudberry preserve, is truly delicious. Cloudberry preserve is also served with pancakes and waffles or used as filling for tårta and almond tarts. A good and easy dessert may be made from sliced sockerkaka topped with whipped cream and cloudberries.

Coffee Bread
Vetebröd

Makes 4 loaves or about
40 rolls

**150 to 200 g (5 to 7 oz.)
margarine or butter
¹/₂ liter (2 cups) milk
50 to 75 g (2 to 2¹/₄ oz.)
yeast
¹/₂ teaspoon salt
1¹/₂ dl (³/₄ cup) sugar
(1 teaspoon ground
cardamom)
1¹/₂ liter or 900 g
(6 cups or 2 lb.) flour**

FILLINGS
   I. **100 g (3¹/₂ oz.) mar-
      garine or butter
      ³/₄ dl (¹/₂ cup) sugar
      ¹/₂ tablespoon
      cinnamon**
  II. **100 g (3¹/₂ oz.) mar-
      garine or butter
      ³/₄ dl (¹/₂ cup) sugar
      50 g (about 2 oz.)
      ground nuts**

GARNISH
**beaten egg
(pearl sugar)**

In a saucepan, melt the margarine or butter. Remove from heat and add the milk. Crumble the yeast into a large mixing bowl, add the salt, sugar, cardamom and milk mixture. Stir in the flour a little at a time and work the dough until smooth and shiny. Cover and leave to rise for 10 minutes in the mixing bowl. Turn the dough onto pastry board and knead it well. Divide in parts and shape into loaves, rolls etc. Let rise on baking sheet until double in size. Brush with beaten egg and, if desired, sprinkle with pearl sugar. Bake the rolls in a 225 to 250° oven for 5 to 10 minutes; bake the loaves in a 200 to 225° oven for 15 to 20 minutes.

Plain Loaves
Släta längder

**1 recipe Coffee
Bread**

Divide the dough in 4 parts. Roll out each part into a rectangle about 20 by 35 cm. Spread with the desired filling. Roll up from the long side and place the roll on baking sheet. If desired, score each loaf with a sharp knife at 1 cm intervals. Cover with a towel and let rise, then brush with beaten egg and bake.

Twisted Loaves
Vridna längder

1 recipe Coffee Bread

Roll out, fill and roll up the dough as for Plain Loaves. Cut each roll in half lengthwise, then twist the two halves together. Let rise, brush with beaten egg and bake.

Butter Cake
Butterkaka

1 recipe Coffee Bread

Roll out, fill and roll up the dough as for Plain Loaves. Cut each roll in 3 cm thick slices and place, cut side up, in a well buttered and floured cake pan. Place the slices about 2 cm apart. Let rise, brush with beaten egg and bake.

Rolls
Småbullar

1 recipe Coffee Bread

Roll out, fill and roll up the dough as for Plain Loaves. Cut each roll in slices 4 cm thick; place, cut side up, on baking sheet. Let rise, paint with beaten egg and, if desired, sprinkle with pearl sugar. Bake.

Saffron Bread
Saffransbröd

1 recipe Coffee Bread
1 egg
1 g (¹/₃ oz) ground saffron

Prepare the dough as for Coffee Bread; take the larger amount of margarine or butter. Before adding the flour, stir in 1 beaten egg and 1 g ground saffron dissolved in a little milk. Shape the dough into rolls, loaves or coffee cakes. To make the special Christmas buns or **julkusar,** pinch off small pieces of the dough and shape into 1 cm wide strips, about 12 cm long. Put two strips together side by and curl in the ends. Stick a raisin into each curl. Let rise, paint with beaten egg and bake.

Fat Tuesday Buns
Fettisdagsbullar, semlor

1/2 recipe Coffee Bread

FILLING
2 dl (about 1 cup)
whipping cream
200 g (7 oz.) almond paste
or
3 dl (1 1/2 cups) whipping
cream
1 1/2 dl (3/4 cup) hazelnuts,
chopped
3 tablespoons sugar

Prepare the dough and shape into 15 to 20 round balls; place on baking sheet. Let rise, paint with beaten egg and bake in a 250° oven for 5 to 10 minutes. Let cool covered with a towel.

Cut a lid off the top of each bun. Fill with a piece of almond paste and cover with whipped cream. Put the lid on top of the cream. If desired, dust with powdered sugar. Or cut a lid and scoop out the inside of each bun. Mix the breadcrumbs with the whipped cream, chopped nuts and sugar; return to the bun and replace the lid.

Quick Rolls
Hastbullar

Makes 16 to 20 rolls

5 dl (2 cups) or 300 g
flour
2 1/2 teaspoons baking
powder
1 dl (1/2 cup) sugar
1 teaspoon ground
cardamom or
2 or 3 grated bitter
almonds
100 g (3 1/2 oz.) margarine
or butter
1 egg
2 dl (about 1 cup) milk
1 dl (1/2 cup) raisins,
2 to 3 tablespoons chopp-
ed candied citron, 8 to 10
chopped candied cher-
ries or 50 g (about 2 oz.)
chopped chocolate

GARNISH
beaten egg
pearl sugar
chopped almonds

Rub the margarine or butter into the dry ingredients mixed together. Beat together the egg and milk, stir into the flour mixture. Add raisins, citron, cherries or chocolate, if desired. Quickly work the dough together and drop into paper cups. Brush with beaten egg and sprinkle with pearl sugar and chopped almonds. Bake in a 200 to 225° oven for about 10 minutes.

Danish Pastry
Danska wienerbröd

Makes 35 pastries.

40 g (1³/₄ oz.) yeast
¹/₃ teaspoon salt
1 egg
2 tablespoons sugar
2¹/₂ dl (1¹/₄ cups) milk
8¹/₂ dl (3³/₄ cups, about
500 g or 1 lb. 1 oz.) flour
250 g (8¹/₂ oz.) margarine
or butter

VANILLA FILLING
2 dl (about 1 cup) milk
2 tablespoons flour
1 egg yolk
1 tablespoon sugar
2 teaspoons vanilla sugar

NUT FILLING
50 g (about 2 oz.)
ground nuts
³/₄ dl (¹/₂ cup) sugar
50 g (about 2 oz.)
margarine or butter

Crumble the yeast into a large mixing bowl, add the salt and sugar. Beat together the egg and milk, add to the yeast. Stir in flour to make the dough firm enough and work it smooth and shiny. Turn it onto a pastry board and knead well.

Roll out the dough to a rectangle about 1¹/₂ cm thick. Cut the margarine or butter in slices and place on ²/₃ of the dough; note that it must not be placed too close to the edge of the dough. Fold the dough in three starting with the plain part. Turn the dough ¹/₄ turn; the "back" of the dough should be facing you. Press lightly with a rolling pin and roll again out the dough to a rectangle. Fold in three. If smeary, let the dough rest in refrigerator for 15 minutes. Turn the dough as before, roll out and fold in three. If desired, chill the dough before rolling out and folding one more time. The dough is now ready to be used for Crescents, Combs and Vienna Rolls. Always let the pastries rise slowly on the baking sheet. Brush with beaten egg and bake in a 250 to 275° oven for 5 to 8 minutes.

To make the vanilla filling, mix all the ingredients except vanilla sugar in a saucepan and bring to a simmer, stirring continuously. Let cool and stir in the vanilla. To make the nut filling, work together the nuts, sugar and margarine or butter.

Combs
Kammar

1 recipe
Danish Pastry

Roll out the dough to a rectangle ¹/₂ cm thick and 30 cm wide. Spread with nut filling or butter. Fold the dough in three lengthwise. Cut in slices 4 to 5 cm thick. Make a few slits at one side of each pastry, bend it a little and place on baking sheet. Leave to rise slowly. Paint with beaten egg end sprinkle with chopped or sliced blanched almonds before baking.

97

Crescents
Gifflar

1 recipe
Danish Pastry

Roll out the dough to ¹/₂ cm thickness. Cut with a pastry wheel or knife in 10 cm squares, cut these in two diagonally. Spread with butter or any of the fillings. Roll up from the wide base. Bend the pastries slightly and place on baking sheet. Leave to rise slowly, brush with beaten egg and bake. If desired, spread the pastries when cool with powdered sugar stirred with water to a thin glaze.

Vienna Rolls
Wienerrullar

1 recipe
Danish Pastry

Roll out the dough to a rectangle about ¹/₂ cm thick and 25 cm wide. Spread with nut filling along the edges and roll up the dough from both of the long sides. Cut in 1 cm thick slices across and place on baking sheet. Leave to rise slowly and bake without brushing with egg. If desired, paint the pastries after baking with water mixed with sugar.

Oatmeal Wafers
Havreflarn

Makes about 30 cookies

75 g (2¹/₄ oz.) margarine or butter
1 dl (¹/₂ cup) oatmeal
1 dl (¹/₂ cup) flour
1 dl (¹/₂ cup) sugar
2 tablespoons light cream
2 tablespoons syrup
¹/₄ teaspoon baking powder

In a saucepan, melt the margarine or butter. Stir in the remaining ingredients. Drop the batter by teaspoonfuls wide apart on buttered cookie sheets. Bake in a 200° oven for about 5 minutes. Let the cookies cool for about 1 minute, then remove from the cookie sheet. If desired, drape the cookies over a rolling pin or similarly shaped object to harden and finish cooling.

98

Sponge Cake
Sockerkaka

2 eggs
1¹/₂ to 2 dl (³/₄ to 1 cup)
sugar
2 teaspoons vanilla
sugar or
grated rind of ¹/₂ lemon
3 dl (1¹/₂ cups) flour
2 teaspoons baking
powder
50 g (about 2 oz.)
margarine or butter
1 dl (¹/₂ cup) milk

Beat the eggs and sugar until pale and thick. Add the desired flavoring, flour and baking powder. Melt the margarine or butter and let cool; stir into the batter. Mix well to a smooth batter. Pour into a buttered cake pan (1¹/₂ liter) that has been sprinkled with fine dry bread crumbs. Bake for about 45 minutes in a 175° oven.

Ginger Snaps
Pepparkakor

Makes about 500 cookies

3 dl (1¹/₂ cups) syrup
4 dl (1³/₄ cups) sugar
1¹/₂ tablespoons ginger
1¹/₂ tablespoons
cinnamon
1 tablespoon cloves
350 g (12 oz.) margarine
or butter
3 dl (1¹/₂ cups) whipping
cream
about 2¹/₂ liter or 1¹/₂ kg
(3 lb. 5 oz.) flour
1 tablespoon baking soda

Stir the syrup with sugar, spices and margarine or butter until well mixed. Whip the cream till frothy and stir into the batter, a little at a time. Dissolve the baking soda in a little water and add together with part of the flour. Cover the dough which should be quite firm, let stand till the following day.
Knead the dough, adding the remaining flour. Roll out a small part and bake a test cookie in a 175 to 200° oven. If the cookie spreads, add a little more flour to the dough. Roll out the dough very thin and cut with cookie cutters into hearts, stars, pigs etc. Let the cookies cool on the cookie sheet after baking.
The cookies may be decorated with white frosting made of sifted powdered sugar stirred with egg white and a few drops vinegar or lemon juice to a thick smooth paste.

Princess Torta
Prinsesstårta

CAKE

Makes about 20 servings

3 eggs
1¹/₂ dl (³/₄ cup) sugar
³/₄ dl (about ¹/₂ cup) flour
³/₄ dl (about ¹/₂ cup)
potato flour
1 teaspoon baking powder

FILLING

2 egg yolks
4 tablespoons sugar
2 teaspoons vanilla
sugar
5 leaves gelatine or
equivalent amount
gelatine powder
4 dl (1³/₄ cups) whipping
cream

GARNISH

225 g (about 7 oz.)
marzipan or
175 g (about 6 oz.)
almond paste + 1 dl
(¹/₂ cup) powdered
sugar + a little
glucose (optional)
green food color
powdered sugar

Beat the eggs and sugar until pale and thick. Mix the two kinds of flour and the baking powder; add to the egg batter. Blend well and pour the batter into a buttered round cake pan (about 2 liter) that has been sprinkled with fine dry bread crumbs. Bake in a 175° oven for 30 minutes. Unmold the cake and let cool. Split the cake horizontally in two parts.

Beat together the egg yolks and sugar for the filling. Whip the cream thick. Soak the gelatine leaves in water, wring them well and dissolve over heat. If gelatine powder is used, follow the directions on the package. Blend the gelatine with the egg batter. Fold in the whipped cream. Let stand until almost set. Put the two cake layers together with part of the filling between. Spread the remaining filling over the top and the sides of the cake which should be somewhat higher in center with sloping sides.

Work the marzipan smooth, or mix the almond paste with the sugar and, if desired, a little glucose. Add food color and blend well to a light green. Roll the marzipan between two sheets of lightly oiled wax paper or plastic foil into a circle large enough to cover the entire cake. Remove the upper paper and turn the marzipan over the cake. Gently remove the second piece of paper. Press the marzipan close to the sides of the cake. Sift with powdered sugar. Store the cake in refrigerator till serving time.

Red Currant Torta
Vinbärstårta

about 1 liter (4 cups)
red currants
sugar
3 round cake layers
2 dl (about 1 cup)
whipping cream

Mix the currants with sugar to taste; stir until slightly crushed. Put the cake layers together with the berries between. Whip the cream thick and spread on top. Garnish with nice clusters of red currants.

A coffee-party table with Christmas Saffron Buns (p. 95),
Almond Tarts (p. 102), cookies and **tårta.**

Almond Tarts
Mandelmusslor

Makes 3 dozen

1 dl (¹/₂ cup) sugar
200 g (7 oz.) margarine
or butter
100 g (3¹/₂ oz.) almonds
5 bitter almonds
4 dl (1³/₄ cups) flour
flour
2 tablespoons cornstarch

Stir the sugar and margarine or butter till light and fluffy. Grind the almonds. Work all the ingredients together and chill the dough for 1 hour or longer. Coat well buttered, small, fluted tart pans with a thin layer of the dough; press with your thumbs. Bake in a 200° oven for about 10 minutes. Let cool for a few minutes, then gently knock the tarts out of the pans. Serve the cookies empty or filled with fruit and whipped cream.

Cheesecake from Småland
Småländsk ostkaka

Makes 10 to 12 servings

8 liter (about 2 gallons)
milk
3¹/₂ dl (about 1¹/₂ cups)
flour
2 tablespoons rennet
8 eggs
4 egg yolks
3¹/₂ dl (about 1¹/₂ cups)
sugar
100 g (3¹/₂ oz.) chopped
blanched almonds
1 liter (4 cups) milk
mixed with light cream
¹/₂ liter (2 cups) whipping
cream

Mix ¹/₂ liter (2 cups) milk with the flour and rennet. Heat the remaining milk to about 35°, then add the flour mixture. Set aside until curdled or about 1 hour. Cut in large pieces and strain through a cloth. Spread the curds in a buttered baking dish (4 liter or about 1 gallon). Beat together the eggs, egg yolks, sugar, almonds, milk and cream; pour the batter over the curds. Stir until well blended. Bake in a 175° oven for about 1¹/₂ hours. Serve warm with fruit preserve. Makes 10 to 12 servings.

Black Currant Mousse
Svartvinbärsfromage

3 egg yolks
1 dl (¹/₂ cup) sugar
¹/₂ liter (2 cups) black currants
4 leaves gelatine or equivalent amount gelatine powder
3 egg whites

Beat the egg yolks and sugar till fluffy. Mix with the berries. Soak the gelatine leaves in a little water and dissolve over heat; if gelatine powder is used, follow the directions on the package. Blend the gelatine with the berry mixture. Beat the egg whites to a stiff foam and fold into the batter. Spoon the mousse into serving glasses and garnish with black currants. Chill before serving.

Variation: Mix black or red currents with whipped cream or stiffly beaten egg whites. Add sugar to taste, chill and serve.

Swedish Apple Cake
Svensk äppelkaka

4 dl (1³/₄ cups) lightly sweetened apple sauce or 6 to 8 tart apples (about 600 g or 1 lb. 5 oz.)
water
sugar to taste
2 to 3 dl (about 1 to 1¹/₂ cups) grated dry, dark limpa (preferably sweet-sour), or finely crushed rusks or bread crumbs
sugar, cinnamon
50 g (about 2 oz.) margarine or butter

Peel the apples and cut in wedges. Cook, covered, in a little water with sugar until soft and mushy. Brown the grated bread, crushed rusks or bread crumbs mixed with a little sugar and cinnamon in the margarine or butter. Butter a baking dish or skillet well and cover with a layer of the bread crumbs. Spread a layer of apple sauce on top, then another layer of bread crumbs and apple sauce. Finish with a layer of bread crumbs. Bake in a 225° oven for 25 to 35 minutes. Let the cake cool a little in the baking dish. If desired, unmold the cake on a serving plate and garnish with sugar. Then cut thin strips of paper and put crosswise on top of the cake. Sift with powdered sugar and carefully remove the strips.
Serve the apple cake with vanilla sauce or cream. Note that the cake need not be baked. Pack the browned bread crumbs and apple sauce in a dish. Let stand for 1 to 2 hours, then unmold.

Fyris Cake
Fyriskaka

125 g (4 oz.) margarine
or butter
1¹/₂ dl (³/₄ cup) sugar
2 eggs
2¹/₂ dl (1¹/₄ cups) flour
¹/₂ teaspoon baking
powder
2 tablespoons light cream

GARNISH
400 to 500 g (14 oz. to
about 1 lb.) soft apples
sugar to taste

Melt the margarine or butter. Let cool and stir with the sugar. Add the eggs, one at a time, then the flour, baking powder and cream. Pour the batter into a buttered round baking dish or skillet (about 1¹/₂ liter) that has been sprinkled with fine dry bread crumbs. Peel the apples and cut in thin wedges; stick these into the batter. Sprinkle with sugar on top. Bake for 30 minutes in a 200° oven.

Rice Porridge
Risgrynsgröt

5 dl (2 cups) water
1¹/₂ tablespoons mar-
garine or butter
2 dl (about 1 cup) regular
white rice
2 dl (about 1 cup)
whipping cream
salt, sugar

In a large saucepan, bring the water to a boil. Add the rice and margarine or butter. Let simmer, cover-ed, for 20 minutes without stirring. Stir in the whipped cream, let simmer for 3 to 4 minutes. Stir now and then. Season to taste with salt and sugar. If the porridge is too thick, add a little milk.
For a not quite as rich porridge, substitute 2 dl (about 1 cup) nonfat dry milk stirred with 1 dl (¹/₂ cup) water for the cream. Add a little grated lemon rind.

MENU
SUGGESTIONS

Luncheons

Thin Pancakes with Pork p. 92 and Lingonberry
Coleslaw
*
Coffee and Oatmeal Wafers p. 98

Grapefruit
*
Fried Plaice with Capers and Beets p. 70
Boiled Potatoes
*
Coffee and Danish Pastry p. 97

Suppers

Swedish Hash p. 76
*
Coffee and Sockerkaka p. 99

West Coast Salad p. 43
Toast and Butter
*
Cheesecake from Småland p. 102 with
Strawberry Preserve

Dinners

Pickled Herring p. 56

*

Beef Patties with Onions p. 74
Boiled Potatoes, Cucumber Salad p. 44

*

Swedish Apple Cake p. 103 with Vanilla Ice Cream

Three Small Sandwiches p. 39

*

Roast Saddle of Reindeer p. 84
Baked or Boiled Potatoes, Tossed Salad

*

Black Currant Mousse p. 103

Perch, broiled   70
Pike, ovenbaked   72
Pike, poached   64
Pike Perch, ovenbaked   71
Pike Perch, poached   64
Plaice, fried with Capers
   and Beets   70
Rollmops   57

Salmon, pickled   66
Salmon Pudding   69
Salmon Trout, smoked
   warm   69
Stromming, Crayfish   61
Stromming, fried   62
Stromming, pickled   60
Stromming, Tarragon   61

Stromming Casserole   63
Summer Casserole   66
Trout, broiled   70
White Lutfisk Sauce   72
Whitefish, broiled   70
Whitefish, ovenbaked   72
Whitefish, ovenbaked Fillets   7
Whiting, broiled   70

MEAT AND POULTRY   74

Beef Patties à la Lindström   75
Beef Patties with Onions   74
Beef Roulades   81
Cabbage Rolls   75
Chicken, fried   86
Chicken Casserole with
   Mushrooms   87
Christmas Ham, ovenbaked   87
Falu Sausage, boiled with
   Horseradish Sauce   77
Game Casserole with
   Red Wine   83

Hunter's Pork   79
Liver Pâté   88
Meatballs   76
Pork, fried with
   Onion Sauce   79
Pork Sauce from Småland   78
Pork Sausage   88
Pork Sausage, boiled   77
Pot Roast   83
Reindeer Casserole   84
Roast Goose   86
Roast Lamb   82

Roast Saddle of Reindeer   84
Roast Saddle of Venison   84
Sailor's Beef   81
Spare Ribs   78
Swedish Beef Stew   80
Swedish Hash   76
Swedish Steak with Onions   80
Veal in Dill Sauce   82

PANCAKES AND WAFFLES   89

Crêpes   90
Crisp Waffles   92

Swedish Pancakes   89
Thin Pancakes with Pork   92

PASTRIES AND DESSERTS   93

Almond Tarts   102
Apple Cake, Swedish   103
Black Currant Mousse   103
Butter Cake   95
Cheesecake from Småland   102
Coffee Bread   94
Combs   97
Crescents   98

Danish Pastry   97
Fat Tuesday Buns   96
Fyris Cake   104
Ginger Snaps   99
Loaves, Plain   94
Loaves, Twisted   95
Oatmeal Wafers   98
Princess Torta   100

Quick Rolls   96
Red Currant Torta   100
Rice Porridge   104
Rolls   95
Saffron Bread   95
Sponge Cake   99
Vienna Rolls   98

REGISTER

109

FOR NOTES